Just A Thought

Reflections on Civic Transformation

Richard A. Johanson

Visit www.booksurge.com to order additional copies.

DEDICATION

To all those who labor professionally or
voluntarily in the public service arena this book
is respectfully dedicated.

Our world will one day be a better place
because of your collective efforts.

* * *

ACKNOWLEDGEMENTS

I wish to thank novelist Bonnie Hearn-Hill for her invaluable counsel in the preparation of this book. Her welcome suggestions and careful editing are deeply appreciated.

I wish to thank Amy Chubb for her ongoing encouragement when I needed it most and for placing me in contact with Bonnie Hearn-Hill.

A special thanks to Howard K. Watkins (www.watkinsphotoarchive. com) for permission to use the cover photograph.

Recognition is also due to all of those unnamed individuals who were the inspiration for many of the thoughts I have tried to express regarding civic transformation.

I wish to thank the design staff at Booksurge for their invaluable assistance and consummate patience.

Finally, I am deeply thankful for all of my family who continue to express their unwavering support of my efforts to make a small contribution to our extended community.

* * *

TO: RICHARD A. JOHANSON

A NOTE OF THANKS ON BEHALF OF YOUR FRIENDS AND YOUR COMMUNITY

Nearly 20 years ago, Richard A. Johanson, while serving as District Governor for Rotary International, made the following statement during the course of a speech to area Rotarians: "Everyone loves a garden, but few will step off its path to cultivate it." The significance of that statement struck me then and now as both a simple truth and call to action. Little did I know at the time that the undersigned, and so many in this community, would be the further beneficiaries of Dick's unique ability to reduce to a few words thoughts both poetic and profound, seemingly simple but of deep meaning, for us to enjoy and learn from over the ensuing years.

In this latest work, Richard has edited and provided a bit of a road map via his "Table of Thoughts", to some of the "Monday Musings" he sent to members and friends of the Fresno Business Council over a 15-year period. This is so typical of the way this humble man thinks – make things simple and easy for someone else to benefit from his work. Take a page from the work of jazz pianist Dave Brubeck who, with long-time colleague and alto saxophonist Paul Desmond, put a good idea to music. "Take Five" from a busy or frustrating day and let your mind focus on a particular title or thought contained in these pages. Apply what you read to the source of your "busyness" or frustration. You will be amazed how often you will bring a new perspective to the task or challenge at hand.

In Richard's first published work, this friend was honored to provide an introduction. A portion seems even more relevant today and is paraphrased as follows:

We are the beneficiaries of these "Thoughts" by our friend, mentor and colleague. We are also privileged to gain a unique insight into his very substance and, accordingly, achieve some understanding of those qualities that make him the person that he is. Confucius said: "Words are the voice of the heart." We take these words from Dick's heart, and as good stewards of that which he has provided to us, have the privilege to apply them today and in the days that follow for the greater good of ourselves our families and the community of which we are a part.

Thanks Dick. May your personal example and words set forth encourage and enable us to "step off the path and cultivate the garden".

The Honorable Robert H. Oliver
February 17, 2009

PREFACE

My story has no beginning, and the ending is still in its formulative stages. Instead, this book is a compilation of fifteen years of observations, compliments, criticisms, and whimsy's. Each heading represents a personal thought as I observed my little part of the world's attempt to transform its stigma as a "Western Appalachia" into becoming a region worthy of recognition because of its dedication to elevating itself to a level deserving of national respect.

In the fall of 1993, the status of public affairs in the central San Joaquin Valley in California, and particularly in the city of Fresno, had fallen to such a low level that they had become a civic embarrassment. Attorney Bob Carter had learned of a concept that originated in Cleveland, Ohio, and was already underway in Stockton, California. It was based upon a premise that a relatively small group of committed individuals with private-sector leadership experience could come together and quietly and effectively spearhead a regional transformation within the public sector. He assembled eight of us to discuss the feasibility of bringing such a plan to our city.

After meeting together a few times we decided to organize a Fresno Business Council. We agreed to limit ourselves to 100 members and quickly filled our self-imposed quota. While our initial focus was centered on public-service issues in the metropolitan Fresno area, subsequent years have expanded our involvement into the surrounding region.

Our ultimate goal was to incorporate the expertise of private-sector management into the public-sector arena on a mentorship basis. Those who had succeeded in high positions of responsibility in the private sector had already demonstrated that they possessed in varying degrees the administrative skills necessary to elevate the conduct of the public's business to the same professional level.

Deborah Nankivell, a lawyer and former regional director of Common Cause in Minnesota, had recently moved to Fresno and was employed by Mr. Carter's law firm. She was assigned by him to assist in the creation of the Fresno Business Council. At its formal organizational retreat, she accepted our offer to become our CEO and remains in that position as this is written. As we entered our second year of existence, I was asked to become president and board chair. I served in those positions for the ensuing five years.

Deborah and I quickly recognized the need to develop an effective method of communication with our membership. From our discussions, we decided to create a weekly FAX Bulletin. It should be noted that Internet e-mail was not yet readily available for such purposes. My contribution was to write an opening paragraph on whatever "Thought" I wished to share with the membership. Deborah wrote the balance of the one-page bulletin. Over subsequent years and by switching to the use of e-mail as the message carrier, the bulletin eventually was distributed to almost one thousand recipients.

What follows is a compilation of selected thoughts written over a fifteen year period. Some of them have been edited to make them more generic in nature. Rather than placing them in chronological order, they have been carefully sorted by subject matter. I would offer a suggestion. The reader may find it more interesting to read this book by selecting a topic heading rather than the usual "front to back" method.

Finally, there are numerous references to our region's broadly adopted "Statement of Community Values." These are the values that contain within them the ethical and moral standards upon which each "Thought" is founded. You will find them listed in the Appendix.

I'm very pleased to be able to share these "Thoughts" with you. Enjoy.

Sincerely,

Richard A. "Dick" Johanson

TABLE OF THOUGHTS

APPRECIATION

A SIMPLE THANK YOU

I like to think in parallels. We all know folks who are facing personal situations oftentimes beyond their capacity to remedy them. There is nothing more appreciated and more comforting than expressions of understanding and encouragement from those who care about them.

It seems to me that there is a parallel here with those who are deeply involved in trying to rectify some of our extended community's problems. Many concerned community stewards are deeply involved in accepting this challenge. As their contemporaries, what if each of us told someone who is toiling so diligently to make this a better place how much we value them?

An "I am thankful for you" takes so little time and can mean so much.

* * *

ATTAINING A VISION

GETTING BACK TO NORMAL

I need to get something off of my chest.

We're hearing a lot these days about "getting back to normal." This country is what it is–this great Central Valley is what it is–our life is what it is–because "getting back to normal" has never been the quest. Within each who calls this place home burns a latent dissatisfaction with the present and an inextinguishable fire to make tomorrow better than today. Where we were yesterday is not a definition of tomorrow's aspirations. Where we are going is a continuation and an affirmation of our heritage. "Getting back to normal" in my book is not a worthy goal.

I feel better now.

* * *

STAYING THE COURSE

When our plate of community concerns is overflowing (and ours is!), our responsibility to ourselves and to those about us is to keep our vision before us and not be detoured into unproductive distractions. We have before us a growing and unprecedented opportunity to become a major catalyst for positive change in a variety of critical economic and social arenas. Proper analysis of important issues, adherence to our core values, a commitment to a collaborative community, and faith in our ability to succeed must be our cornerstones. One day this region will reflect upon how we accepted our responsibilities and acted upon them.

Kind of exciting, isn't it?

* * *

ACCEPTING THE CALL

One of life's biggest challenges, it seems to me, is recognizing one's personal responsibility to dedicate effectively discretionary time to productive community service. The farther we travel along our journey as extremely busy people, the more important it becomes for each of us to define and accept our role in striving to attain our common vision. Where are we? Can we do more or are we already at capacity? The need is great Working together we can meet it.

It's a tough call that confronts each of us..

* * *

STEPPING UP

Here's my favorite new phrase: "Stepping up." Ideas are great. Plans are fundamental. Good wishes are welcome.

However, unless there are those who are willing to step up, all is for naught. A day does not pass in which we are not made more aware of the growing willingness of folks to move from talking the talk to walking the walk. The more our efforts at improving things around here are made known, the more "step up" types will join us with an offer to help. Chances are you're one of them.

And that's a huge step forward!

* * *

GETTING THERE

One of the strengths of those committed to creating change is their ability to stay focused on mutually agreed upon goals. Candid discussions in group settings about different approaches to resolving emerging concerns are concluding with unanimity of purpose.

Throughout this process we are witnessing a determination by the participants to stay the course in seeing that all of those sub issues vital to the creation of a vigorous local economy are addressed effectively. Our goals are attainable and our commitment to attaining them is awesome!

We're getting there.

* * *

ARTISTS AT WORK

What if we looked at all of our efforts to make this a better place through the eyes of an artist? While we are neither a Monet nor a Dali, neither are we Bozo the Clown.

Landscape artists from all segments of our greater community are in the process of creating an exciting new montage combining the realities of today with the dreams of tomorrow. As we continue to create our own masterpiece, let's not undermine our effort with faint-hearted brush strokes.

Michelangelo didn't.

* * *

DEFINING OUR QUEST

The other day I was thinking about this region's vision of transforming itself from Good to Great. The immediate question became refining the definition of a "vision." Is it a vague pipe dream? Is it an esoteric academic concept? Is it just one more scribbling on a flip chart? Is it merely a PowerPoint attention grabber?

Or is it a commitment of dedicated community stewards who deeply believe that, by coming together in a noble cause, we can transform ourselves from the nation's Western Appalachia into a region worthy of national acclaim for our collective acumen? Our vision is noble. Our vision is attainable. Our mission is inspiring others to pursue our vision with us.

* * *

SEEKING OUR TOMORROW

Do you ever notice how often we encounter unforeseen pitfalls in our ongoing search for solutions to some of our most pressing issues? It is out of resolving such potential roadblocks that we are discovering new, exciting and effective ways of meeting many of the social and economic challenges confronting this part of our world. A clearly defined vision among those who are committed to a better tomorrow for our children and grandchildren is the fundamental driver of the momentum required to bring us success.

As someone so elegantly put it, *"You must be moving to stumble."*

* * *

A SWEDISH PROVERB

One of my uncles (A Swede, of course!!) was fond of saying: "Too soon old, too late smart." I yust figured out vy ve are getting smarter. Since I vas yust a little towhead folks around hyar have been creating Vision Statements vich de vould frame and hang on a vall. Now ve are enfolding our Vision within our hearts and minds....

Yumpin yiminee, no vonder ve are getting smarter. I tink my uncle vas trying to say: *"We Need To Think Differently Rather Than To Try Harder."*

* * *

COLLABORATION

THE PATHWAY TO SUCCESS

Our extended community is watching with pleasure the public-agency castle caretakers draining more water from their moats, ignoring the threats from the alligators, and further lowering their drawbridges. They are recognizing that joining together in a broad spirit of jurisdictional collaboration is rapidly replacing narrow minded civic isolationism as the pathway to tomorrow's economic strength in California's great San Joaquin Valley. They are beginning to realize that it is the health of the entire kingdom that will make those who reside within it individually stronger. We have discovered that organizational connectivity is the pathway to a better tomorrow. Unfortunately, at the same time, we are witnessing those agencies whose vision remains impaired because of their self-imposed isolationism being left behind or made irrelevant.

Tomorrow's successful social and economic policies must be sound in concept, solid in principle, broad in vision, mutually supportive in purpose, consistent in funding, and innovative in execution. Such is our collective pathway to success.

* * *

STRENGTH IN WALKING TOGETHER

For some time, the focus of this region has been centered primarily about those activities concerned with the New Economy and our place in it. While we retain that focus, we are now witnessing an exciting expansion of our vision by increasingly concentrating on broader community efforts. As we go through this process, we are accepting that there are differing views among us regarding the most effective ways to reach the same goal.

It reminds me of the old story of two youngsters, each struggling to retain his balance while teetering down parallel railroad tracks. They suddenly discovered if they but reached across to each other and joined hands, they would support each other, and their walk would become stable. There is no more deserving expenditure of time and talent than that devoted to our mutual welfare. Therein resides the strength of walking together.

* * *

FINDING NEW EYES

I heard something thought provoking the other day: "A voyage of discovery is not seeking new landscapes, but finding new eyes."

Does it seem to you that the excitement of our voyage as community stewards is growing because we are finding new eyes in working to solve the problems confronting us? Are we not more willing to find answers to our challenges through each other's eyes as well as our own? In doing so, aren't we creating an innovative revitalization of our existing landscape rather than trying to construct a new one? Ultimately, aren't we all embarked upon a unique voyage of discovery together? I think so.

* * *

SEEING THE LIGHT

As we travel along our journey into this new century, certain expressions are becoming ever more commonplace in our daily vocabulary. Words such as communication, collaboration, regionalism, inclusiveness, (feel free to add some more) come readily to mind. Some of us grasp their significance as easily as turning on a light switch. To some of us, these expressions are akin to using a rheostat. Regardless of how we come to see the light, our journey to progress will ultimately be determined by our ability to illuminate our goals and follow the lighted pathway to attainment.

* * *

CORE BELIEF UNITY

One of the most fascinating observations in the transformation of this place from Good to Great is appreciating the ability of those individuals and organizations with differing viewpoints on surface issues to come together because of the unity of their core beliefs. They have shunted aside pettiness, jealousy and expediency in favor of creating well conceived programs and policies designed to ensure constructive non-polarizing results. A strong commitment to a common success by unselfish leaders working together is the motivator for the changes we are witnessing all about us.

Think of it this way: "Those who row the boat don't have time to rock it."

* * *

THE REAGAN LIBRARY

Recently I had a chance to visit the Reagan Library in Simi Valley. I brought home one of President Reagan's quotations. "There is no limit to what a man can do or where he can go if he doesn't mind who gets the credit." (Excuse the masculine gender.)

I think this is the reason those involved in transforming this region have been able to reach their present level of intensity, integrity and respectability. Numerous public agencies are working as an unselfish unit in seeking to fulfill a common mission.

So the question becomes: How do we instill President Reagan's words into the minds of some of our elected officials who oftentimes seem to place personal recognition above collective public progress?

* * *

GANG MEMBERSHIP, Aug. 19, 2002

I think there is a kinship building around here unlike anything seen in many years. It's like a giant club. You can even call it a "gang" pointed in the right direction. It has an ever expanding membership open to all who wish to join. Its members greet one another in quiet appreciation of each other's contribution to its growing success. Its activities cover all sectors of our society. Its aspirations reach to the sky. Its foundation is deep in our being. Its membership is comprised of those dedicated individuals and organizations among us making a difference.

The next time you meet someone who is also committed to making this a better place for all of us, greet a fellow gang member.

The concept is sort of neat, huh?

* * *

TEAMWORK

Most of us are intrigued by comparables.

Watching the Fresno State Bulldogs play football recently, I was struck by the correlation between a team's win/loss record on the gridiron with community and regional successes and failures. Player recruiting, inherent talent, and a fire-in-the-belly determination to succeed are the fundamental ingredients without which the most grandiose game plans are doomed to fail.

The success of this extended community in its aspirations for a new tomorrow will be attained as a result of establishing a sense of teamwork. No single coach, no single player, and no single lineup, can bring home a winner without the dedication and active participation of all of those comprising the team. For verification, check out the organizations and individuals making a difference in this region.

Shake hands with your teammates.

* * *

RIDING THE RAILS

Have you ever considered that traveling within the parameters of a democracy is akin to riding the rails in a passenger train? One rail supports the leadership qualifications and standard of conduct by those who serve us. The opposite rail supports the community standards we have set for ourselves. Whether the rails run in a straight line or must go around a curve, as long as they remain parallel, our system of government functions efficiently. It is only when the distance between the rails is altered for political expediency that our journey as passengers is endangered. It is up to us as journeyers to insist that the tracks remain parallel.

All aboard, please...

* * *

UNCLOGGING OURSELVES

Our shower drain hasn't been working too well for a while. The other day, with a little coaxing from my plunger, it started to drain a bit better when all of a sudden whatever was causing the clogging gave way. Now the water just swishes through the pipes. Sort of makes one see an analogy to all the good stuff that is beginning to happen in this area, doesn't it?

We're becoming unclogged!

* * *

PRIVATE-SECTOR PARTICIPATION

One cannot make an effort to be in tune with all that is going on in this region without acknowledging the strong motivation for change that is emanating from the private sector. Committed and knowledgeable individuals and organizations within both the private and nonprofit arenas are enlarging their interaction with public sector resources. We still have a long road to travel, particularly in the areas of poverty, job creation, and education. However, we are beginning to see significant improvements. We know the direction in which we are going and we are on the move. We are not standing idly by waiting for an external elixir of some kind that will solve our internal problems for us. And that is good.

* * *

ACKNOWLEDGING PROGRESS

Have you noticed that this region is rapidly undergoing an interesting transformation? Not too many years ago we were the seekers of outside wisdom in addressing a long list of societal problems. Today we are witnessing a growing number of instances where we are being sought for advice on the creative ways in which we are solving these same problems.

The credit for much of this significant turnaround must be shared among volunteers and committed staff personnel of numerous organizations who have come together in a common cause. Their enthusiasm in seeking success in their individual arenas deserves our deepest gratitude. They are staying the course on behalf of all of us.

Good stuff is happening, and it isn't a local secret anymore.

* * *

COMMITMENT TO ACTION

I remain fascinated by all of the positive happenings taking place among us. In earlier times, good people would come together and hold meeting after meeting and eventually create a concept paper for proposed change that would promptly be filed away while everyone diverted their attention to something else on the immediate horizon.

What we are seeing now, in my opinion, is that our actions include a heretofore missing ingredient. Fundamental is a commitment to stay the course by the participants.

Passiveness is passé. An active contribution is expected. Inherent is an expectation of adequate time for individual contemplation and study followed by a group created measurable action plan specifically designed to attain specific goals. No longer is merely sitting in a meeting room and discussing noble aspirations while making sure not to disturb the status quo considered a productive use of anyone's time. One needs only look at the current committees, alliances and personal relationships among those with overlapping concerns to witness this exciting transformation.

Hopefully, our regional history will one day contain a small footnote that the Fresno Business Council, of which I am proud to be a member, was a leader in creating this new regional aura of economic, social and educational enhancement. To all of those who saw the vision and acted upon it, we owe a tremendous debt.

* * *

OBSTACLES – "I" VERSUS "WE"

Do you know what can be an obstacle to trying to improve things around here? It is that some among us still think they are an island unto themselves. Without acceptance and resolution of differing viewpoints, as well as acknowledging one another's strengths and weaknesses, they are easily deluded into the quagmire of thinking "the only right way is my way."

As this region moves forward, it is imperative that we do so as a cohesive body of concerned citizens committed to a brighter tomorrow for everyone. Not only is it a heckuva lot safer, but the ensuing exhilaration and comradeship is downright contagious. "We" can do it.

* * *

CROSSWORD PUZZLES

Do you like to work crossword puzzles? I do. In any case, consider this. The horizontal words represent the continuity of the public sector. The vertical words represent the depth of the involvement of the private sector. This great Central Valley is solving larger and more difficult puzzles every day because of our growing adeptness in understanding that both facets must interface properly to bring about lasting solutions.

* * *

FOCUS

It's all in how you look at things.

Consider the progress this region is making in so many arenas. Here is a paraphrase of something I heard last week that hits
the point head on: "When you focus on the things that unite us,
you can resolve those things that divide us. When you focus on the
things that divide us, you destroy those things that unite us."

Whether one calls it unity or collaboration, we are creating a
common focus dedicated to the betterment of a united community. We grasp the clarity of our vision and have it well in sight.

* * *

COMMUNITY HEALTH

HEALTH CARE CONCERNS

Nothing is more basic to the success of an organization than a healthy work force. Businesses, particularly, cannot be healthy entities without healthy employees. Because of our oftentimes unhealthy air quality, this region needs to be especially involved in the wellness of all who are among us. A recent report showed that Fresno County spends approximately $2 billion dollars annually on the treatment of chronic diseases which result in absenteeism and reduced productivity.

It is not the purpose of this thought to advocate a particular program but to bring attention to the benefits to be derived from focusing on health care issues such as smoking cessation, fitness incentives, health screenings, obesity, diabetes, and high cholesterol. As we say in the business world, the investment is cost effective.

* * *

MUNICIPAL MEASLES

Last week I drove by an inoculation center for children about to enter school. As a kid, did you ever have the measles - full of nausea on the inside and covered with ugly red sores on the outside? I think that our extended community is rapidly getting over a case of municipal measles.

Internally, discourtesy is being superseded by dignity. People from all segments of life are uniting in an aura of mutual respect in seeking to solve difficult social and economic problems.

Externally, we are witnessing almost daily an emergence of projects designed to remove our blemishes. The application by the City of Fresno to receive an Empowerment Zone designation and the creation of a new Juvenile Justice Campus are but two examples.

One day soon, all that will remain is to ensure that we are vaccinated against re-infection.

* * *

COMMUNITY VALUES

SETTING OUR COMMUNITY STANDARDS

In this person's humble opinion, no self-adopted document has made a greater impact on what is going on around here than "Community Values of the Fresno Region." Because of our collective refusal to accept less than the best from ourselves, we are well along on our journey to becoming nationally recognized as a community capable of private/public civic transformation.

Adhering to our "Community Values" is our litmus test for progress and is helping us discover the space where self interest and common interest can come together. Ultimately it all comes down to this: *"Ethics Is Obedience to the Unenforceable"*

* * *

SEEKING A HIGHER QUALITY OF LIFE

As we pursue our quest for local and regional quality of life enhancement, it is important that we reflect from time to time upon our unique characteristics. To cite just a few examples:

We are a culturally fragile population.
We reside within a depressed economic area.
We have a K-12 school system that needs major attention.

These, and other pressing issues, have embarked us on an inspired crusade for change. We are moving forward because we have unselfishly acknowledged who, what and where we are. We have committed ourselves to arriving at a better tomorrow. Out of commitment comes fulfillment.

* * *

FACING OUR FUTURE

One of the truisms of those of us who are getting older is an increasing awareness of the importance of staying focused on common goals and not become overly distracted by differences on how to attain them so long as all options meet our adopted "Statement of Community Values."

All about us are individuals and projects dedicated to bettering our community. All around us are collaboratively minded organizations equally committed to the "cup half full versus cup half empty" approach. Together we are creating a new horizon based upon those values we have established for ourselves today as the bedrock upon which to build our tomorrows.

* * *

COMPELLING ISSUES

WATER WOES, A SCARY SCENARIO - 1998

Do you know what's scary around here? It has been the reluctance of the "Queen City" of the San Joaquin Valley to look its water usage problem squarely in the eye.

Fresno, California, is one of only four major cities in this nation that does not monitor (aka water meters) residential water usage. Its current water resources are precarious. Its population will double in the next twenty years. Its present pumping facilities are inadequate (particularly in the older parts of the city) and costly. Its available sewage treatment facilities are woefully incapable of meeting tomorrow's demands.

This entire region needs to ensure that its finite water supply will remain sufficient for tomorrow's population, for its farms and for its businesses (aka jobs). In particular, the city of Fresno needs to adopt the same water conservation measures taken by other progressive cities throughout this land. It must act decisively today to make certain that tomorrow's generations will not become parched victims of yesterday's unconscionably selfish short sightedness.

Does it have the will? That's what's scary!

* * *

RIDING AN UPSWING, 2005

It has occurred to me that our collaborative processes in improving our community are much like the Dow Jones Index—there are periodic downturns but the long-range trend has historically been upward.

Recently we have seen the creation of a new coalition group by the Mayor of Fresno, a renewed commitment by Fresno County with significant support from the City of Fresno and the private sector regarding the Elkhorn Juvenile Justice Correctional facility, the formalization of the Joint Powers Authority between Clovis and Fresno Unified School districts with strong input from the Business Council to open and jointly operate the upcoming Center for Advanced Research and Technology (CART) as a lab-based school for high school juniors and seniors, the resolution of the dispute on the structure of the Fresno City Redevelopment Agency, just to name a few things.

In my opinion, our stock is a good buy.

* * *

THE NEW ECONOMY, 2000

We're devoting a lot of energy at the present time to both an internal and external analysis of how best to maximize our effectiveness as we enter what is becoming known as the age of the "New Economy."

Nothing better describes the potential impact of this New Economy than an article I read last week. Here is just an excerpt: "An explosion in spending on information and communication technologies is having a profound effect on the ways economics work. The impact could be significant enough to warrant comparison with the British Industrial Revolution and its later counterpart in America. The evidence increasingly suggests that the world economy might be in the early stages of a third industrial revolution. Today's 'once-in-a-century acceleration in innovation' (Alan Greenspan's words) has the potential to raise productivity and economic growth significantly above their long-term trends. This phenomenon could last for two decades or more".

Our challenge is to stay on the cutting edge of progress into this new era Do we have the will?

* * *

THE NEW INVESTORS

I would like to share a thought taken from a book entitled Return Flight by Robert D. Lupton:

"Compassionate people with marketplace savvy are beginning to enter the public arena with ideas and strategies that challenge the failed wisdom of the status quo. Along with their optimism, they work with words such as *development, accountability, partnership, responsibility,* and *effectiveness.* They are a new generation grounded in marketplace reality, accustomed to risk-taking, and unimpressed by rhetoric. They have tasted the American dream and have seen that pursuing possessions without compassionately investing one's self in service yields a lack of fulfillment. For the first time in recent history there is a growing movement toward involvement that calls for significant self investment."

That's a thought worth remembering.

* * *

CULTURE

CULTURAL DIVERSITY

I was reminded once again last week about the privilege of being an American and living in an open democratic society. I attended a meeting at which we were presented with information on our cultural similarities and differences. All too often too many of us expect everyone to be a clone of a single cultural cookie cutter. We forget that our cultural ancestry is steeped in traditions that have been carried into this land by those who have emigrated here since the formation of the United States of America. (Even the Swedes brought some stuff, albeit not a heck of a lot!). Read again the inscription under our Statue of Liberty and be inspired: "Give me your tired, your poor, your huddled masses".

* * *

ARTS TO ZOO - 2000

We recently witnessed an incredible exhibition of what can be done when people of concern and commitment for our quality of life, particularly as it lays the foundation for our children, become the cornerstone in building a stronger tomorrow for all who live in this great Central Valley.

Our cultural institutions, from the majors such as the Chaffee Zoo, the Fresno Metropolitan Museum, the Fresno Philharmonic, Artes Americas, the Afro-American Museum, The Fresno Historical Society and the Fresno Art Museum to those who are or can become an integral part of the cultural arts within our smaller communities such as the Selma Arts Center, the Kerman Arts Council and the Shaver Lake Historical Society, have united in a never-before-seen spirit of cooperation to work toward passing an Arts to Zoo 2000 initiative that will appear on the November ballot. Individuals and organizations who normally work on a fee-only basis are volunteering their skills to join the campaign. Throughout Fresno county individuals who care for our quality of life are surging forward wanting to know how they can be a part of this great effort.

There is excitement in the air from the Arts to the Zoo.

DEMOCRACY IN ACTION

GOD BLESS DEMOCRACY, OCTOBER 2001

This thought may run a bit long. Please bear with me.

One of the tenets upon which our regional transformation is based revolves around relationships between the private sector and the public sector and in particular the elected public sector. Mutual trust, highest ethical standards and compatible goals are the primary prerequisites needed to create an invigorated local economy. Fundamental to success will be our ability to persuade highly qualified individuals of unblemished character to seek public office.

In recent years, we have witnessed almost daily examples of embarrassing conduct by some inept elected officials bent solely upon attracting unwarranted attention to themselves. Spurred on by the Fresno Business Council, in concert with other organizations of like-minded purpose, there came about the "Election of the Century" in which each candidate for public office was asked to sign a pledge regarding his/her campaign conduct.

As a result of that effort, this region, and in particular the City of Fresno, saw a marked change in the way most subsequently elected officials conducted themselves both while seeking office and while serving in their elected positions.

Unfortunately, recently we have witnessed the evolvement of an embryonic campaign by a prospective candidate for public office in which the hoped for higher standards of conduct and character are in danger of being trampled once again. This candidate has made numerous false statements regarding prior knowledge and implied approval of his unethical conduct by both private and public citizens duped into accepting prominent positions of campaign support on his behalf.

It is to the credit of the city of Fresno's highest elected official, Mayor Alan Autry, and several members of the Fresno Business Council, also finding themselves in the same paradox, they also removed their names from the campaign in keeping with the platform of high moral and ethical standards expected from public office candidates.

Democracy is the noblest experiment in self-government ever created. Where tarnish exists, democracy will remove it. Where tarnish is threatened, democracy will prevent it. Where tarnish is forbidden, democracy will prosper from it.

* * *

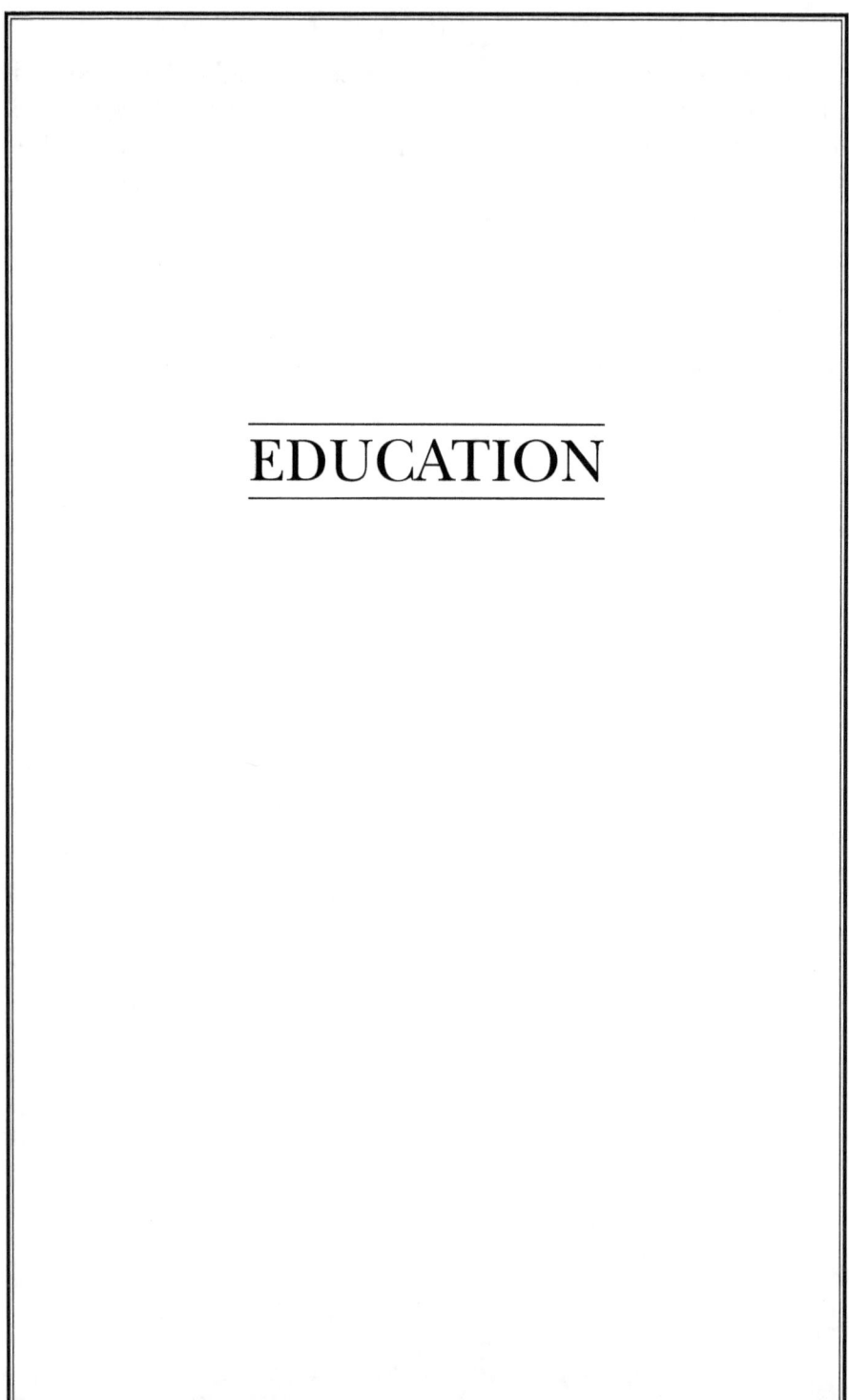

EDUCATION

ATTAINING EDUCATIONAL EXCELLENCE

The struggles within our educational system at all levels have been an interest grabber for years. We are all aware of the issues involved. So, what does it take to make our system perform at its best? Every Super Bowl Sunday, two excellent football teams prepare to face each other. We might find within them an answer. No single coach or group of assistant coaches, no quarterback, no player at any position, no stadium of supportive fans, can become a winner without successful teamwork on the field of play.

While we shall always have laggards among us, our greater community is realizing that if we are to attain our potential, we need a strong focus on maximizing the quality of education provided to students at all levels. This community's support for education is based upon this single premise – assembling and motivating a system-wide integrated and supportive team of dedicated players at all positions. When we accomplish that, we'll be in the Super Bowl of Educational Excellence.

* * *

REINVIGORATING A SCHOOL DISTRICT

One of the earliest identified attention areas of those seeking regional transformation in our Central San Joaquin Valley was job creation. Fundamental to this aspiration is the availability of an educated work force. In recent months, there have been significant improvements within the formerly troubled Fresno Unified School District under the leadership of new Superintendent Michael Hanson. He is being strongly supported by a revamped Board of Trustees as well as by community-based individuals and organizations including the Fresno Business Council. Critical to the success of these changes is the performance of the teacher in the classroom. *Accountable empowerment* is the new buzz word in the Fresno Unified School District.

The future looks promising.

34

STAYING THE COURSE

It is time for all of us to contemplate how much positive momentum is underway in our local K-12 school system because community organizations and individuals of differing positions on substantive issues have been able to come together in a spirit of open-mindedness to arrive at mutually acceptable solutions.

Two specific examples are career education and addressing youth violence. All of this progress is premised around providing a better tomorrow for those who will follow us. We are learning as we go that our future depends upon the willingness of our entire community to come alongside our educational system. Our kids and grandkids are depending upon us to stay the course.

* * *

THE CENTER FOR ADVANCED RESEARCH AND TECHNOLOGY

Recently many of us witnessed the dedication of the Center for Advanced Research and Technology. The C.A.R.T. came into being because the Clovis and Fresno school districts realized that by working together they could create an outstanding satellite educational institution that neither could underwrite alone.

Contrast this with the "almost final" approval last week for the creation of a downtown Fresno multi-purpose stadium. After almost eight years of persevering against mind-numbing obstructionist tactics that need not be reviewed here, the super majority of the Fresno City Council at long last sent forth a clear message-they, too, want "collaboration and cooperation for our common betterment."

With the opening of C.A.R.T., our local school districts are showing our extended community leaders that working together is the doorway to progress.

* * *

AN APPLE A DAY

School bells have once again signaled the start of another year heralding the magic of education.

Why don't we take a few minutes to reflect upon our debt to all of those who labor so intensely to ensure that our kids receive the knowledge base they will need to propel them into a satisfying and productive lifetime? To school boards, superintendents, administrators, support personnel and, most of all, our teachers, our community thanks you for your devotion to your accepted responsibilities. Particularly to the Fresno Unified School District, we offer our appreciation for your return to fiscal integrity coupled with an absolute commitment to devote as many assets as possible to the classroom.

Finally, we owe a debt of gratitude to those community volunteers who have given so freely of their time and talent to come alongside our educational professionals on behalf of our kids.

Let the school bells ring. They are the music of a brighter tomorrow.

* * *

GRADE-LEVEL READING

The past few weeks have been a time of personal meditation about our young people just beginning their educational experience. I suggest that all should set some time aside to focus on the future awaiting our first, second and third graders. For many of these community treasures, the challenge of learning to read at grade level is a tall mountain to climb. Currently in Fresno, almost two-thirds of our kids score below grade level. It is predicted that over ninety percent of this group will not attend college. We can help change this.

ReadFresno is one of our pathways to progress. Through participating ourselves and encouraging others to become readers/mentors for one hour per week, through the donation of books, and through assisting in funding for program staffing and supplies, we can make a lifelong difference in a child's life.

Here's the best part—we can make a difference in own lives too.

* * *

EDUCATIONAL CODE OBSERVATIONS

Being of Swedish ancestry, it sometimes takes things longer to sink into my skull than it does the rest of you. So, explain something to me please.

Why, when educational leaders, both elected and appointed, parents, community members of all shapes and sizes, analysts and others all agree that the way in which education is delivered to our kids is seriously flawed in this state, do we continue to accept the status quo? Why, when we already have twelve volumes of educational "code," did our legislators, in seeming direct contrast to the wishes of those named above, propose five to seven hundred new pieces of legislation this year directed to education? The Commission on the Future of Education in Fresno County, co-sponsored by the Fresno Business Council and the Fresno County Office of Education, proposed some extensively researched answers several years ago including addressing the cumbersomeness of our Education Code. It is this fundamental—the people want simplification of mandates influencing their kids' educational opportunities. Maybe it's time to join hands and create our own protest march to our state capitol. As someone once said: "If not here, where? If not now, when? If not us, who?"

* * *

K-12 KIDS – A COMMUNITY'S PRIDE

Let's devote a few words to our K-12 kids. From the Civic Education Network, to Character Development programs, to Pre-school programs, to After-school programs, to One-on-One mentoring, to Libraries, to the influence of Music and Drama, to the discipline of Sports activities — thousands and thousands of our kids are growing to young adulthood in an environment conducive to a healthy and productive life style. It is from this cadre that will emerge men and women who will have within them the benevolent fire to one day seek ways to help those less fortunate than themselves because of the help we are providing for them during their school age years. There is no higher legacy we can leave for our kids and grandkids.

I can only express one person's admiration and gratitude to all of those involved in the education of today's young people. A simple "thank you" seems woefully inadequate, but it will have to do.

* * *

SCHOOL BELLS ARE RINGING

If there is one identifying theme as each September prepares to greet us, it is the realization that our schools are beginning another year of providing a life-lasting education to our young people. Each fall we witness a renewed focus on the educational requirements of our students and the level at which our various systems are meeting them. The public has become rightfully indignant over past failures and generously complimentary over measurable successes.

Despite ongoing funding stresses, there exists a new aura of determination both within and without our educational community to improve the scholastic achievements of our youth. What for too long was an "us versus them" mentality is rapidly evolving into a "we" spirit of collaboration.

To which our kids can only smile and say: "It's about time."

* * *

EDUCATION AND ELECTIONS

Have you considered that one of the real conundrums of any election year is the inferred assumption that all of us are uniquely qualified to vote on extremely complex issues? As in every election year, no legislative initiatives nor office-seeking campaigns will be of greater importance to our future than those revolving around education. Educating our children effectively requires that we first educate ourselves thoroughly as voters.

Of prime importance is the need for all of us to take the time necessary to inform ourselves about those who are seeking School Board positions. What are their qualifications? What are their motives? What are their visions? How will they interact with teachers, administrators and students?

The answers are on our ballots. Our kids are depending on us.

* * *

OVERCOMING HARDSHIP

Last Friday morning I attended the graduation ceremony of our second granddaughter from the College of Social Sciences at CSUF. It was an impressive event.

That same afternoon I was privileged to attend the ribbon cutting of the new Juvenile Justice facility for Fresno County. It was there that I listened to the testimony of Carissa Phelps. She described her life as a homeless 12-year-old. She was in and out of Juvenile Hall. She told us she attempted suicide when she was fourteen. Thanks to a caring correctional officer and an "extra step" teacher from the County Office of Education, she has turned her life around. She is now working on two advanced degrees at UCLA.

As we attend graduation parties among our families and friends this season, it behooves us to remember those graduates who have survived personal hardships that most of us will never fully understand. May our efforts as part of a caring community help inspire those whose names we shall never know but whose lives we may forever touch.

* * *

SYSTEMIC EXCUSES? - COOL IT

One of the good things going on around here is an intense focus on our educational system. Here are a few suggestions as we go forward.

Rather than Ph.D.-type Doctoral Dissertations on Dysfunctional Developmental Disciplines, why not more Vocational Ed-type Dialogues on Disappointing Test Scores? Why not less orating in the harshness of a press conference spotlight and more discussion in the softness of a classroom's illumination? Why not less pontification and more collaboration?

Folks are saying, "We know it's broken, and we are determined to fix it – together." Our community is telling us that it cares about its kids and wants to do better. And our kids are telling us "that's cool!"

* * *

ACHEIVING EXPECTATIONS

A hot-button topic lately concerns the performance of our educational institutions. We are refining our expectations of them and their ability to meet those expectations. Recognizing well publicized budgeting restraints and despite contentious vocalizing by those who would polarize vital issues, there exists a circle of dedicated educators and community volunteers who are working diligently to mitigate differing positions to ensure that our children receive the best possible education we can provide for them. To these passionate community icons we owe a deep debt of gratitude.

Lest we think that such problems are of recent vintage, I remind you of a statement attributed to a fellow named Aristotle which reads: *"All Who Have Governed Become Convinced That Our Future Depends On the Education Of Our Youth"*.

Three cheers for Mr. Aristotle!

* * *

ELECTIONS

WHY ELECTIONS IN THE FALL?

I just figured out why we hold elections in the fall. Outside my window stands a majestic maple tree with its leaves all draped in red and gold and yellow in preparation for its wintertime hibernation. All of us witness this annual October transformation thankful for nature's spectacular seasonal gift of vibrant color. At the same time, we are assured that in a few short months we shall welcome the annual spring time excitement of emerging bright green leaves out of the void of winter's dormancy.

So, too, it seems to me, do we witness this same cycle through our election process. Whether some leaves drop silently from the tree shriveled and forgotten, or whether they glide gracefully earthward shimmering in all of their departing glory, their time is at an end. Shortly they will be replaced by new growth bringing with it a sense of renewal and optimism for us all.

And that is why we hold elections in the fall!

* * *

ELECTION DIMENSIONS

Someone once made an observation that you can't control the length of your life, but you can control its width and its depth. We are now in the middle of our democratic ritual of participating in the election process. We are more carefully analyzing candidates for office. We are more studiously scrutinizing ballot issues. We are more faithfully exercising these prized privileges as concerned voters.

All about us we are witnessing a new dedication to reaching a higher economic, cultural and moral plateau collectively. In other words, we are increasingly assuming our fair share of the responsibility of controlling the width and depth of our lives as we journey through its uncontrolled length.

As my English professor said one time, *"that ain't all bad."*

PUBLIC/PRIVATE SECTOR PARTNERSHIPS

One of the great truisms we are learning in our journey to transform this region is the interconnectivity of symptoms. Caring without acting is simply an emotional exercise. Acting without an integrated plan is wasted energy. "Strategy without tactics is the slowest route to success. Tactics without strategy is the noise before defeat," said Sun Tzu. As a region, we are making significant strides in addressing economic, social and infrastructure issues. The private sector's involvement is a critical component. Ultimately, effective solutions must comprise focused human and fiscal resources from the public sector.

As we go forward, we need to ensure those who are campaigning to become our elected leaders possess the administrative skills and the personal commitment fundamental to alleviating these societal stresses. If they fail, it is our failure also as an electorate.

* * *

STRONG LEADERS

Pass the cookies, please. I just figured it out.

We talk an awful lot about seeking "strong leaders" and encouraging them to become part of our political process. Problems arise when a candidate or office holder uses the two words together. The individual involved becomes inwardly focused as a self-described strong leader. Real leadership comes when the two words are considered separately and focused externally. For example, "strong" defines one's ability to recognize the value of the contributions of others through collaborative knowledge, cross-cultural awareness, and socio-economic variances. "Leader" defines one who can move among peers and accept unsought recognition for his/her abilities in moving common goals forward. As we evaluate those in public office, it might be well that we keep these separate definitions in mind.

Is that worth a cookie or not?

* * *

TAKING THE 'I' OUT OF POLITICS

Here is a little sidebar thought as we take a brief respite from the upcoming political campaigns.

Let's declare the vertical pronoun unacceptable. There is no "I" in "Government". Ours is a government of the "People" which has no "I" either. Our task in the coming months is to select those persons we believe are most qualified to conduct our local, state and national symphonies while recognizing that the baton by itself makes no music. What We the People need are maestros most able to inspire each of us to perform our best as participating musicians.

A final thought—there is no "I" in "maestros" either.

* * *

DEFINING LEADERSHIP

One of the rewards of being privileged to periodically record one's thoughts during the election season is the opportunity to express one's opinion on candidate qualifications. One may agree or disagree but, hopefully, each reader will find this thought worthy of contemplation.

The topic for this week is leadership. During the upcoming campaigns, we shall be overwhelmed by those who wish to be our leaders. Each office seeker will provide us with their individual definition of what leadership means. It will be up to us to correlate the candidate's definition with our own. Such an analysis precludes that we have a clear definition of leadership in our own minds.

What's yours?

* * *

EXPECTATIONS

Now that our public officials have all made their anticipated pledges to represent all of the people during their upcoming terms of office, perhaps the time has come to expect more than traditional rhetoric from them. Extremism on both sides of the political spectrum is rapidly being relegated to irrelevancy. From our Governor's commitment to work with all people to the public commitments by emerging national leaders to walk a middle ground, we are witnessing a window of opportunity for a significant social and economic transformation.

The Fresno Business Council has been a frontrunner in its ongoing advocacy for the abolishment of bureaucratic and philosophic silos as well as increased interaction between the private and public sectors. It would appear that the lights are being turned on. The doors are opening. We're preparing to enter tomorrow's world together.

* * *

JUDGMENTAL FAIRNESS

Let's talk about judgmental condemnation for a second. Have you noticed how easy it is to be critical of the administration of a public body? We often forget that within all public organizations exists a cadre of highly dedicated knowledgeable professionals whose responsibilities are to carry out policies presented to them without prejudice.

As we enter the final months before Election Day, we should caution ourselves to avoid unwarranted blanket censure of those employed in the public sector. There is wheat. There is chaff. Let's not mix them up.

* * *

CAMPAIGN STANDARDS

As we go through our bi-annual election process, our focus must not be diverted from our core values by slick campaigns. We cannot reach our sought-after goals without a strong body of highly qualified elected leaders. We shall one day be measured by our ability to work with all of those whose aspirations are compatible with ours while respectfully disagreeing with others. We shall be judged by our commonality, not our diversity. We need elected officials who will place the common good above personal pedestals and place truthfulness above distortion.

It is right that we expect knowledge, dedication, integrity and dignity to comprise the core characteristics of those who would represent us. As the campaigns move forward, these must be the standards by which campaigns are measured.

* * *

ASSESSING CANDIDATES

As we watch those who are considering becoming candidates for political office in the new year, it is interesting to observe how they view themselves. Are they asking for election because of their professed individual ability to have all of the answers to all of the problems facing us? Or are they running for office because of a desire to become a leader/servant willing to work with all segments of our society based upon a deep rooted conviction that out of such collaboration will emerge a stronger community?

Our increasingly involved electorate, it seems to me, is responsible for establishing dramatic new expectations of those who would seek our support for public office. We are demanding abandonment of an egocentric "I" philosophy to an understanding of the validity of an authentic "We" posture. To our fellow voters who are responsible for this attitudinal change, we owe each other a big thank you.

* * *

A POLITICAL PARADOX

What's your position on paradoxes? Webster says a paradox is an assertion seemingly contradictory but that yet may be true in fact.

In these exciting times, so many are searching for ways to come together for the common good. Nowhere is this commitment stressed more strongly than by candidates for public office. At the same time, it is a major league paradox that candidates for public office advocate their search for this unity by stressing their differences with each other and those not supporting their candidacy. Their ultimate test will be the elimination of the paradox should they be selected for public leadership.

Our challenge, both individually and collectively, is to keep ourselves focused sharply on the goals we have established for ourselves while working in conjunction with our public and private sector allies. And that's no paradox.

* * *

A POST-ELECTION OBSERVATION

Once again, the caring citizens of this country have expressed their preferences on candidates and issues through the ballot box. To all those men and women who have been elected to represent us in varying capacities in the upcoming years, we offer congratulations. It is in these newly elected and re-elected individuals that we place our trust for a better tomorrow. Elections are recommitments by our citizenry to our never-ending aspiration for an ever-ascending standard of excellence on the part of those who would govern us.

May the promises our office holders made in seeking office now become their mantra while serving in that office.

* * *

A POST-ELECTION ALLEGORY

I would like to paraphrase an allegory that I heard the other day.

Now that the elections are over, it is important to recognize what we have done. We have retooled the governmental vehicle that transports us by carefully inspecting its current roster of drivers (aka office holders) and making any changes that we deemed appropriate. We have updated and reprogrammed the engine that drives it by adjusting its current components (aka ballot measures) as we saw fit.

What we have not done, and cannot do in the voting booth, is use the ballot box to provide the propellant that is fundamental to both of these components. Without energy to activate it, our transporter is merely an inert beauracratic creation. Each of us must now reaffirm our responsibility to provide our share of the energy needed to move ourselves forward.

* * *

POST ELECTION REFLECTIONS, 2001

Congratulations to all of those newly elected public officials who are just completing their traditional one-hundred-day honeymoons. We particularly congratulate City of Fresno Mayor Alan Autry for his superlative effort to bring his city together again through his willingness to work with all segments, his vision in presenting new concepts for debate, and his tact in agreeing to disagree with dignity.

Consider this: When this year started there was but a single high-rise construction crane in downtown Fresno. Its use? The city is constructing another jail. How many cranes will grace the skyline by the end of this year: stadium, hospital, courthouse, hotel, Save Mart Center, and others? We have replaced "we can't" with "we can." We have turned a corner on our highway to excellence as an extended and caring community.

* * *

FACING CHALLENGES

THE NEW ECONOMY

The New Economy – Mark it down. Study it. Welcome it.

We are participating in the birth of an economic revolution. How we accept it will determine the future of our region for decades to come. The backbone of the transformation going on about us–collaboration, regional thinking, better education, improved public safety, qualified public administration–is also the backbone of the New Economy.

As railroad tracks join together in the distance, so our regional vision will become one with the realism of the "New Economy" as we move forward.

* * *

GRASPING THE CHALLENGE OF CHANGE

I think that one of the greatest challenges of community betterment organizations is the temptation to become so caught up in the work of today that many lose sight of their mission as the transformation agents of tomorrow.

Recently, selected community members had the privilege of participating in a session sponsored by the California State University system designed to develop an action plan to chart this region's course for the future. Three of these strategy meetings were held throughout the state. The assembly included representatives from across the San Joaquin Valley, many of them graduates of one of the twenty-three schools in the CSU system. Like other transformational work, the focus included issues that would impact every educational institution in the network including areas that need customized programs because of local demographics and unique economies. The conclusion and our ultimate challenge is to balance the needs and responsibilities of individuals with those of their communities.

Through this window of opportunity lies the vision of a new tomorrow.

TRANSFORMING EXPECTATIONS INTO REALITY

I sense there is a new buzzword in the air around here. It is "expectations". Busy folks no longer are amenable to spending their valuable time sitting in meetings just to discuss "stuff." Our emerging energy-charged atmosphere translates into a demand for the formulation and execution of action plans arising out of innovative agendas.

It is the expectation of positive measurable results that is creating a new meeting room culture hereabouts. Busy community-minded business leaders have been the front runners in this transformation. They are laboring collaboratively throughout our greater community to raise our expectations of who we are and what we can accomplish. Their visionary efforts will ensure that today's dedication will contribute to a better tomorrow.

* * *

FAITH IN TOMORROW

We spend a lot of time thankful for the significant progress already made promoting existing programs in numerous arenas in our part of the world because of the commitment of such organizations as the Fresno Business Council and its many partners.

What we don't discuss as often is the incubation and hatching of new programs that will support and accelerate our ongoing regional transformation. These fledglings will fly because of our deep-down belief that good things happen when good people unite for a good purpose.

All of this is my sneaky way of leading up to an old Scandinavian saying: *"Faith Is a Bird That Feels Dawn Breaking And Sings While It Is Still Dark."*

* * *

CLIMBING OUR MOUNTAIN

As we refine our mountain climbing expedition up a variety of trailways designed to improve the economic and social environment of this region, ponder this.

A host of community partners now have realistic visions of a attaining a higher than originally expected elevation. The route to this new summit is admittedly difficult. Much effort is going into preparation for the scaling of this lofty height. New routes are being studied. Innovative strategies are being evaluated. Time lines are being determined.

Alas, and almost predictably, there are some who now have trepidations about the altitude and who now wish to delay or divert our commitments to our aspirations. It reminds me of an old saying: *"Obstacles Are the Problems You See When You Take Your Eyes Off Of the Goal"*.

We have a mountain to climb. Let's scale it together.

* * *

MEETINGS, THEIR PURPOSE

Let me tell you about two meetings I attended recently—back to back.

In the first, the participants spent the first hour and thirty minutes listening to "expert" opponents negatively listing even the remotest of reasons why a proposed public/private agreement could not be made workable. Not once in this time frame was there any reference to collaboratively searching for alternative solutions. In the second, there existed a spirit of cooperation among public and private sector representatives as to how a great program can be made even better through strong cooperation.

In the first, there existed postures based upon personal aggrandizement. In the second, there existed a spirit of mutual respect and unity of purpose.

In the first, there was a pall of "just listen to our position and do as we say." In the second, there was the satisfaction of knowing that all viewpoints should have the opportunity to be heard and evaluated, and that the best ideas would be used as the basis for moving forward

Two meetings back to back–two different worlds.

* * *

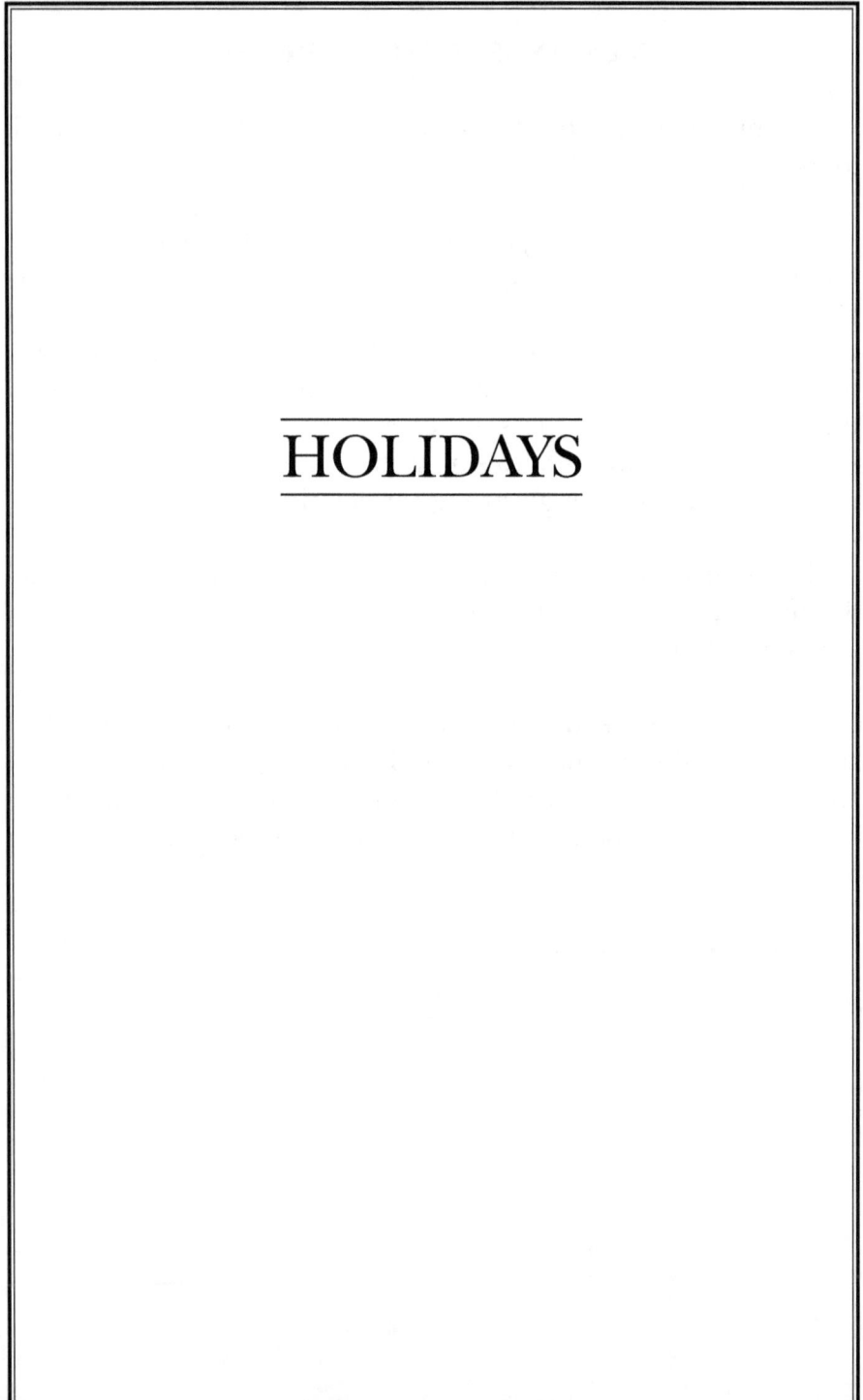

HOLIDAYS

SPIRIT OF A NEW YEAR–JANUARY 1997

Would you like to know what one of the most exciting things on my mind is as we enter another year? We are on the leading edge of a new spirit of collaborative effort among private and public organizations dedicated to creating an improved social and economic life for all of us. Let's take a look at a few examples. The Clovis Unified School District is working ever more closely with its sister educational entities and creating stronger alliances with the private sector. The members of the Fresno County Board of Supervisors are working with the Fresno Business Council and others on job retention and creation. The Mayor of the City of Fresno is working with a community-based advisory committee on the proposed downtown stadium.

We are witnessing a growing conviction that by combining our expertise we shall arrive at better solutions to community opportunities (not problems.) We shall be refining our strategies as to how best to take advantage of the challenges before us. We need the input of everyone. There is a spirit of hopefulness in the air. A New Year is at hand bringing with it a deeper understanding what we can accomplish by working together.

* * *

A "CAN BE' NEW YEAR, 1998

As we enter another year as advocates for an improved quality of life for all of our people, I wish to share a thought I picked up while watching a video with my four-year-old granddaughter over the holidays. Somebody said "Some people look at things and see them as they are. Others look at things and see them as they can be." What a powerful statement!

Our challenge as we enter this New Year will be to define how things "can be" and chart our course to get there. We must find ways to increase our economic, moral and cultural strength while eliminating or reducing those divisive issues which confront us. While individuals may disagree passionately on some issues, our ultimate strength lies in respecting and learning from our differences while maintaining unity behind our common goals.

I sense that implied in all of this lies the basis for a community-based New Years Resolution. Our immediate challenge is to draft it.

* * *

WELCOME TO A NEW YEAR--2002

Somewhere in the excitement of the all of the newsworthy events that are taking place in this region rests a fulcrum. We are all riders on a gigantic seesaw. I would offer that we are now beginning to relish the view from the up end after our vision has been obstructed for much too long on the down end. When we consider all that is happening hereabouts–downtown Fresno revitalization, medical facilities expansions, the Collaborative Regional Initiative, educational institution growth, business retention and expansion incentives, etc., it is obvious that we are entering a new year on a significant upswing. What is occurring is the result of a broad-based private/public commitment to create an improved civic environment for the betterment of all of us.

Let's join together in congratulating all those involved in placing us on the high end of the teeter-totter. A reminder–let's not fall off.

* * *

HELLO TO 2008

Another year is ending, and a new one is just beginning. It is now time to contemplate our individual and organizational opportunities to increase our transformation contributions in 2008.

Recently I was given a wonderful little book entitled "*The Velveteen Principles.*" I submit the following quotation as our 2008 mantra: "*Generosity does not involve handing over boxes tied with ribbons. Instead, it is an expression of a certain spirit of goodwill and encouragement. When we are generous in this way, we support people when they need us most, not when it is most convenient for us.*"

May our New Year be filled with compassionate generousity.

* * *

PRESIDENT'S DAY REFLECTIONS

Here's a thought about Presidents Day.

When we think of former presidents whom we hold in high esteem, what are the factors that influence us? Is it because of the passage of significant legislation, healthy economic growth or other external factors occurring during their term of office? Or is it the inherent character of the individual? I respectfully submit that it is both competence and character.

In that line, I believe that same standard applies to all of those who seek public office at any level today. Therefore, I suggest that as we consider those whom we shall support, we measure each of them against those past Presidents whom we hold in highest regard It is our responsibility to establish our expectations It is up to today's candidates to assure us that they can meet them. Our most esteemed past Presidents did.

* * *

VALENTINE'S DAY

Valentine's Day to me is as inspiring and as fresh as the beauty and the fragrance of a dew covered rosebud. It is a wonderful day devoted to expressing to those whom we cherish dearly our love for them and what they have brought into our lives.

How about adding a variation this year? Why don't all of us use this day to celebrate our appreciation of our greater community? It is out of our devotion to this place we call home that so many continue working so diligently to make it better. You can even call it love.

* * *

EASTER'S MESSAGE OF HOPE

Every spring the Christian world celebrates Easter and its biblical assurance of an eternal tomorrow. It seems to me that, in addition to its religious significance, Easter can also serve as a holiday of temporal assurance of a better tomorrow right here at home. I believe men and women of compassion everywhere carry within them an unquenchable thirst to help create a better life for everyone. It is this overt concern for others and a compulsion to help bring about positive changes that drives each of us individually and as a part of a highly motivated extended community to stay focused on a common ultimate objective–a better tomorrow.

May the full Spirit of Easter abide within each of us.

* * *

EASTER CONTEMPLATIONS

No one can witness the significance of the Easter Season without endorsing an aspiration that tomorrow can be better than yesterday. None of us, of whatever theological belief (or lack thereof), can escape the message that individually and organizationally we have an obligation to improve ourselves at the same time that we work to assist those about us. If we accept such a premise, we are then left with a choice. Do we become active participators or do we become sedentary observers? To put it another way: *"Character Doesn't Come From Circumstances, It Comes From Choices."*

* * *

MEMORIAL DAY, 2002

One of the strongest assets of this great country is our ability to take time from the hectic pace of our daily lives to reflect upon the significance of our major holidays. Of these, none is more American than Memorial Day.

Why don't we each set aside a few moments for meditation this week? Let's resolve to exhibit to those around us the vitality of our national and personal core values, particularly in relation to each other, as we address the difficult issues before us. In doing so, we are paying the ultimate respect to our nation's departed heroes.

God Bless America, Land That I love.

* * *

HOORAY FOR PATRIOTISM

The Fourth of July is our great Holiday for celebrating our patriotism: parades, "The Stars and Stripes Forever" (Thanks Mr. Souza!), fireworks, band concerts, picnics, hotdogs and hamburgers, baseball. For this we can thank our forefathers for creating a government of, by, and for the people.

Hereabouts you can feel the excitement for progressive change in the air led by an increasing alliance between the public and private sectors. It is only when those in office misinterpret this aura by seeing themselves, rather than the people, as the government that we seem to wobble a bit. More and more we are joining together in a parade of pride. I feel like marching. Do you?

* * *

THE FOURTH OF JULY

Every year America honors with speeches, parades and fireworks our founders whose vision and dedication gave birth to this great nation. We honor those of moral courage who placed the responsibility of lasting public service above immediate personal gain. Today they are recognized for their contributions from pictures on our currency to names on our streets and schools.

This year why don't we pause and personally honor today's heroes who toil anonymously in the trenches of volunteer service without receiving or seeking public recognition? This year why don't we find a way to say thanks to someone whose volunteerism is equally unselfish in such tasks as docents, aides and readers in institutions such as our museums, our hospitals and our schools? These are the quiet people who daily sustain what our famous forefathers began so long ago. No speeches, no parades, no fireworks—just a heartfelt "thank you."

P.S. While we are honoring those who have gone before us, let's not forget to remember Betsy Ross for creating our flag.

* * *

LABOR DAY BUS DRIVERS

If there is a common thread among successful collaborators, it is their advocacy for interaction and leveraging of resources among agencies. People and organizations have lowered their drawbridges and drained the moats around their castles. We are becoming fellow travelers on an enlightened journey. What we are witnessing is a regional economic, cultural and educational transformation that is attracting nationwide attention. Regrettably, those few individuals and organizations who continue to espouse the "go it alone" route are being left behind.

As we prepare to celebrate our national holiday honoring all of those who toil so hard to contribute to our common welfare, what better way to celebrate Labor Day than to give thanks to those who are riding in the bus that is moving us along.

* * *

LABOR DAY'S OPPORTUNITIES

Once a year this nation pauses to recognize all of those who labor in recognition of their contribution to the bedrock of this nation. Whether in our industries, our educational institutions, our farms or our professional and community services, it is appropriate that we dedicate a special day in their honor.

As we prepare for the challenges of meeting the Regional Jobs Initiative's goal of 25,000 new jobs in the next five years, educators, employers and prospective employees will need to work in keen cooperation to create the needed qualified work force. No longer can management and labor be looked upon as opposing ends of our economic development chain. To create our "tomorrow", they must be linked closely together. Theodore Roosevelt said it best: *"Far and away, the best prize that life has to offer is the chance to work hard at work worth doing."*

Happy Labor Day to all.

* * *

A THANKSGIVING THANK YOU

As we approach Thanksgiving Day, I would like to paraphrase an old poem:: "How do I love you? Let me count the ways". Let's change the wording to "How do I thank you?"

I am thankful for family and friends without whom
there would be no rewarding life.
I am thankful for those willing to commit time and resources to help the less fortunate.
I am thankful for the privilege of living in a land where westrive to resolve differences without rancor.
I am thankful for all of those community-based organizations who subscribe to the "Statement of Community Values"
I am thankful for the assurance that a better tomorrow is at hand throughout our region because so many care so deeply.

* * *

THANKSGIVING 1997

As we prepare to celebrate another Thanksgiving holiday, the thought occurs to me that our nation's traditional November theme of "Thanksgiving" might serve us well as a theme for the fourth anniversary of the founding of the Fresno Business Council.

For four years this council has been able to increase its impact as a relatively small group of business and professionally oriented men and women committed to working for better public/private collaboration. It seems to me our "Thanksgiving" should be not only for the benefits we are beginning to witness as a result of this coming together, but also a "Thanksgiving" for the opportunity given our members to contribute to our society as a whole.

* * *

THANKSGIVING DAY, 2002

How about trying something different this year? Rather than celebrating a Thanksgiving for what we have, how about celebrating a Thanksgiving for what we don't have?

Those of us who will be dining at a bountiful table aren't homeless. We don't live in poverty. We don't struggle with language and customs in a strange land. We don't lack an adequate education. We don't live in a dysfunctional home environment. We don't lack friends whom we can rely upon for comfort and counseling. You get the idea.

Let's give this a thought on a day devoted to thanks giving while we're enjoying the turkey and pie. We have so much to celebrate, and so much to share!

* * *

THANKSGIVING 2005

On Thursday our nation will pause to celebrate a contemplative day of Thanksgiving. Our history lessons tell us that it all began when our country's founders gathered with Native Americans to express appreciation for their safe deliverance to this new land.

It is right that every year we set aside a special day to recognize our sense of divine gratitude as a free nation. Individually, each of us can use this day to meditate upon our present blessings while continuing our efforts to make our part of the world a better place. Each of us can use this day to give thanks for all of those dear to us. It is a day for joyful reflection.

I thankfully share these words of contemplation: " *"Thanksgiving Is Not The Fulfillment Of What You Want, But The Realization Of What You Already Have."*

* * *

WINTER TIME WARMTH

Do you feel a special glow all about us at this time of the year?

It seems to me that this brief time between the reflections of Thanksgiving Day and the emotions of the upcoming Christmas and New Year's Day holidays is filled with an aura all of its own. There exists within and around us an enlightened sense of concern for others, an analysis of our recent accomplishments and disappointments, and a calm acceptance of tomorrow's challenges.

We all bask in the assurances provided by so many dedicated individuals and organizations that are an integral part of this halo of oneness. Let us be thankful for what we have done and be prayerfully hopeful that we shall successfully meet those challenges that lie ahead of us.

It's a wonderful time of the year.

* * *

A CHRISTMAS WISH, 1998

As this week progresses most of us will join in the tradition of exchanging gifts with those who are close to us. My wish at this Christmas time is that as the beautiful bows, the colorful ribbons and the bright paper are removed from our gifts to each other, each of us will find under the outer packaging the inner spark of compassion and love without which a gift becomes only a sham.

May our gift to our greater community be one of deep concern for the betterment of all of our brothers and our sisters. May we recognize that ultimately it is neither the wrapping nor the content, but our inner admiration for each other that makes each carefully decorated package become a lasting treasure.

* * *

THE SPIRIT OF CHRISTMAS, 2001

In view of the world changing events of the past year, I would like to share with you once again my thoughts as first expressed on December 22, 1995.

"AT CHRISTMAS TIME does it seem to you that:

We are more tolerant and appreciative of each other.
We are more thankful for our families and our loved ones.
We are more compassionate to those in need.
We are more conscious of our earthly finiteness.
We are more cognizant of the true meaning of the Season.

It does to me."

As our world grows smaller day-by-day, may our faith in our abilities to meet its increasing challenges grow larger hour by hour...

Happy Holidays each and every one.

* * *

CHRISTMAS COMARADERIE, 2003

I received a very moving little book last week all about friendship. It gently reminded me that our ongoing Christmas season celebration is focused around a divine friendship. I believe our daily challenge lies in transferring this seasonal aura into a year-around atmosphere of personal trust and commitment. Such is the bedrock upon which our lives rest. Such is the foundation upon which we are building our effectiveness.

My hope is that we shall each set aside a private time every day to reflect upon those whom we cherish as family and friends. May the Blessings of Christmas and Hanukkah be among you. May the New Year reward you with happiness and peace.

* * *

GOODBYE 1995 – HELLO 1996

As time passes by, I have an ever increasing cognizance of the opportunity for betterment of our greater community because of the determination of committed leaders within involved public and private agencies. Each day brings news of the exciting and many faceted activities of their work for the common good.

One dominant thought keeps coming back to me. The approaching new year is going to be pivotal in the improvement of our social and economic environment. Our efforts as business and professional leaders, together with alliances among a growing number of supporters from all sectors of society, are going to create a refocused electorate, a cooperative and energetic public staff, and a reinvigorated private sector. It is countdown time until the green flag drops signaling the beginning of another transformational year.

1996 will begin with our concentration on the roadway ahead of us and our accelerator pressed to the floorboard.

* * *

INSPIRATION

INSPIRATIONAL LEADERS

Surely one of life's greatest gifts is that of being inspired. The wonder of inspiration brings with it a passion to emulate those who, by their strength of character, their high ethical standards, their openness to dialogue and their steadfastness of purpose, create within us a conviction that life does have a higher plateau which can be reached by each of us if we but seek it.

By whom have you been inspired? Have you told them so lately?

* * *

ESPIRIT DE COMMUNITY

It is always interesting to contemplate what inspires individuals to give generously of both their positional and discretionary time in an effort to create a better society about them. All of us know many who fit into this category. They are immensely deserving of our admiration. I believe it is this "espirit de community" that is giving rise to the formation and success of the regional transformation going on all about us.

I hope you feel it too.

* * *

WINTER OLYMPICS, 2002

You know what I like about the Olympics? We get to use words like "torch" and "venues." They fit right in with what is going on right here at home.

We're all emerging Olympians engaged in a gigantic multi-faceted contest to improve ourselves. We're all striving for an economic and social Olympic medal for this region. We're all carrying a flaming torch which is casting a brilliant glow over this place. Each of us has our own special venue in which to make a valuable contribution to our overall team effort.

The only question remaining is the color of our medal. I'm betting on Gold.

* * *

OPTIMISM FOR THE FUTURE

It's extremely difficult not to get caught up in comparisons sometimes. Consider all of those addressing many of our rightful concerns in this region versus those who can only castigate. From denigrating our business climate, to lambasting our K-12 school system, to bemoaning the needs of our underprivileged, we have no shortage of cynical critics.

What has been missing and what is emerging is an ever-growing number of committed visionaries with the skills to bring about change. We have adopted a united vision of where we are now and where we want to be tomorrow. Most important, we have identified the path we must walk to get there.

As Helen Keller said a long time ago: *"The Only Thing Worse Than Not Being Able To See Is To Be Able To See And Have No Vision"*

* * *

ARTICHOKES

Do you like artichokes?

This thought hit me at the super market the other day. How long since you pondered (Swedes ponder a lot) that an artichoke is nothing more than a thistle turned benevolent? We are all leaves on the bulb of our choice? We have the option of being part of a bedraggled thistle bearing bush destined to dry up and blow away, or we can be leaf on a nutrition-filled artichoke deriving strength from a common heart. I think what we are creating around here is a whole field of artichokes.

Ralph Waldo Emerson said it this way: *"What Lies Behind Us And What Lies Before Us Do Not Compare With What Lies Within Us."*

* * *

RECIPE FOR COMMUNITY GROWTH

My mother loved to collect recipes. What do you think of this one her son created for garnishing community involvement?

A dash of Public Affairs
A pinch of Educational Concerns
A drop of Agri-Business Development
A jigger of Job Creation
An ounce of Crime Control
Stir well—season as desired—partake at will

* * *

THE "WEs" ARE WINNING.

I have come to believe that there is one criterion by which we may measure ourselves as we continue to surge forward in our commitment to elevate conditions around here. Among those who are really participating in the hard stuff, there is a marked absence of the word "I" and a marked increase of the word "We." The "We" people are the ones reaching out to all segments of our society and inviting them to participate in this rewarding effort through a variety of collaborative processes. The attention seeking self-focused "I" folks are becoming irrelevant.

Check it out and see if you don't think "we" are in agreement.

* * *

TRUE GRIT

Who remembers John Wayne in "True Grit'?

"True Grit" was everywhere among over three hundred folks totally immersed in the creation of a new tomorrow for this region at the Fresno Convention Center recently. These dedicated folks have decided that we now have the determination and the resources to meet our current economic and social challenges head on. We shall do so by a carefully crafted program of job creation coupled with an educational program ensuring that we have among us qualified individuals to fill emerging jobs. No longer are we just mouthing words. A new spirit of resolve is all about us.

"True Grit" is back!

* * *

NOSTALGIA

What's your opinion of nostalgia?

In a conversation the other day, I heard someone long for the "good old days." My unspoken reaction was that the "good old days" have a place in historical records and fond memories but that for living, vibrant and concerned citizens our focus needs to be on the "bright new future."

While nostalgically reminiscing about days of yore may provide fond memories, it is the future and our work towards its betterment that will bring us our maximum satisfaction. It's worth a thought.

* * *

INVOLVEMENT

COMMUNITY ENGAGEMENT

One of the challenges in inspiring others to become involved in community activities is finding a way to vividly illustrate the impact of their efforts.

At a recent meeting an artistic friend put his brush to the canvas! Discussing our dedication to moving this region from "Good to Great", he explained how everything is related to Community Engagement. What he was telling us is that understanding our interconnectivity is the easel supporting the panoramic mural we are creating all about us.

Do you get the picture?

* * *

DISCRETIONARY TIME

Last week I had a stimulating conversation regarding one's use of discretionary time. We all know those who feel guilty if they are not constantly engaged in a productive activity. Others believe that free time is a "no guilt" opportunity to spend as the moment dictates.

Somewhere within these parameters lies the commitment of members of this extended community who are deeply involved in its transformation. Most of us have first call obligations on our time. How we wish to spend our discretionary time is a personal decision for each of us. It is to the credit of so many of our community builders that they have decided that a portion of such time should be spent in seeking a higher quality of life for all of those among us. To each of them we owe a deep debt of gratitude.

* * *

MOTIVATION

A GROWING EXCITEMENT

Isn't it intriguing how we can all become so excited about such spectator events as baseball or football or basketball? Our hearts beat faster. Our adrenalin output increases. We become emotionally involved. What is equally exciting to me is the growing and enduring participation of all of those involved in the hands on event of reinvigorating our own extended community. Job creation, social issues, school performance, civic infrastructure, just to name a few, are matters of concern that are attracting growing numbers of dedicated individuals and organizations.

The increasing excitement is all about us. It could be called a community-based adrenalin rush.

* * *

ATTITUDE THEN APTITUDE

It's simply not possible to participate in some way with the progress being made around here in community development without wondering what is making it tick. Here's my thought. We have always possessed the aptitude for change but for far too long lacked the attitude. People and agencies concerned with jealousies, pettiness, personal aggrandizement, turf, etc., all have varying levels of a disruptive attitude within them. It is only when a transformation in attitude becomes an integral part of a collaborative process that aptitude begins to change into effectiveness.

To our credit, we're adapting our aptitude to our attitude.

* * *

LIGHTENING WITHOUT THUNDER

What do you think of this? "Thunder is impressive because of its noise, but it is lightening that shows us the way".

It seems to me that the destiny of civic leaders is to serve as a lightening rod on community betterment issues. It is not their function to be debaters wherein one side must win and the other side must lose. Rather, their mission is to act as facilitators striving to identify the best of both sides and reach effective amicable conclusions. They are visionary participants in an emerging collaborative and illuminated society. The combative thunder of "kill or be killed" is passé. Light, not noise, will guide us into tomorrow.

* * *

NATIONAL COURAGE

COURAGE, SEPT. 11, 2001

On Sept. 11, 2001, we witnessed incomprehensible acts of terrorism resulting in an unwarranted slaughter of hundreds of innocents in New York City, Washington, D.C., and Pennsylvania. At the same time these despicable deeds ignited indescribable acts of courage.

I would ask all who read this piece in remembrance of that day's tragedy to create within themselves an expanded reservoir of personal courage: courage to continue resolutely on our path to create a better society for all, courage to resolve sharply differing opinions in a calm and rational manner, courage to comprehend that we are all one in God's universe and courage to clasp all whom we love closer to us.

May God bless courage.

* * *

A REFLECTION ON SEPT. 11, 2001

I think the most striking aftermath of the Sept. 11 holocaust has been the ability of this nation to come together in a spirit of determination to eradicate the terrorist threat to our freedom. People of all races, faiths, and political spectrum have discovered that their differences pale almost into insignificance when placed against their similarities. They are united regarding their determination to protect our system of government for all of our citizens. It is good that we have differences. What is not good is when they become distractingly strident.

May each of us in our own lives continue to demonstrate that building bridges is the answer to our social and economic growth. May we strive always for construction rather than reconstruction.

In our time of grief, we are discovering once again that we are a United States of America.

* * *

OUR HOLOCAUST ONE YEAR LATER – INNER STRENGTH

As we remember this nation's holocaust of one year ago this week, permit me to add a thought or two. As we outwardly wave our flags and listen to speeches this week, why don't we take a little extra time to look inside ourselves and rediscover the foundation upon which this nation came into being.

The United States of America was created on a premise that peoples of differing ethnicity, talents, and philosophies could come together under a single flag to share a common dream of brotherhood. Despite periodic daunting challenges, that dream still exists as does the resolve to attain it. It is deep within the marrow of our bones and the pulsing of our blood that we find the sustenance which drives us forward in our day to day efforts to create a better community for ourselves and for our world.

As we outwardly exhibit our patriotism this week, let's not forget it is our oftentimes unspoken inner strength that unites us.

* * *

NATURAL DISASTER: HURRICANE KATRINA, SEPTEMBER, 2005

The devastation brought on by nature's power in Louisiana and Mississippi will be noted by historians for generations. Never before has nature so devastated a portion of our nation. As this is written, thousands remain without possessions of any kind.

My wife and I just returned from a couple of weeks in Northern Europe including revisiting the scene of a WW11 "scorch the earth" area in northern Norway the size of the entire nation of Denmark. I was vividly reminded of the power of people to overcome indescribable hardships whether created by man or nature.

We, too, shall overcome our tragedy because *"A Nation's Greatness Resides Not In Her Material Resources But In Her Will, Faith, Intelligence, And Moral Forces."*

81

WONDERS OF THE WORLD

Recently I witnessed an indescribably beautiful sunset standing on the south rim of the Grand Canyon. While worldwide geological treasures are created by nature, the thought occurred to me that many of the man-made wonders of our world are equally as impressive. Edifices such as the Great Wall in China and the Pyramids in Egypt are perpetual gifts to each of us by thousands of unknown toilers whose names we shall never know.

Here at home on an admittedly miniscule scale, all about us are examples of selfless individuals and organizations who are coming together in creating our own regional wonder. My thoughts are filled with admiration and appreciation for their many contributions to the lives of those who will follow them but will never know them.

If we but stay the course, one day people will look upon this place and silently express thoughts of gratitude to those civic heroes who anonymously gave so much to make our small part of our world a wonder in its own right.

* * *

CHATTING WITH THE REDWOODS

One of my anticipated joys upon the arrival of springtime is making a pilgrimage to the Giant Sequoias in Kings Canyon National Park. To stroll, pause, and meditate among these nearly two thousand-year-old redwood trees is to fully appreciate our brief space in time. As one gazes skyward at their outstretched branches, they appear to be thanking us for our ongoing efforts to elevate and perpetuate our own personal and community values.

As we continue on our journey to create a better world for all among us, we need only heed the message being sent to us by these ancient sentinels—"our task is not to reach a destination but to create a better pathway for those who will follow us".

I urge you to take a trip up into the nearby Sierras and have your own private chat with these inspiring natural treasures. Tell them Dick sent you.

* * *

PERSONAL COMMITMENT

THE NEEDS OF THE KINGDOM

Once upon a time a group of knights, all busily involved in their own part of the forest, became seriously concerned about affairs throughout the kingdom. So they got together and formed a council to discuss ways in which they could collectively help make the kingdom better. They quickly realized that if they took a more active interest in the process of selecting those to lead the kingdom that things would become better for everyone in the forest. And so each knight assumed a rightful share of the challenge of enhancing the way the kingdom operated.

The challenge remains with us within our own forest. What is our fair share of responsibility for the affairs of our kingdom?

* * *

VOLUNTEERISM

How many hours did you spend in volunteer committee meetings last month? I think that one of the major changes going around here is that those who are willing to devote a portion of their work day to volunteerism are increasingly recognizing that meetings just for the sake of meetings are a waste of their time and talent.

Nonprofit staff leaders are recognizing that if they ask busy people to serve as volunteers, they must demonstrate that the service being asked is worthy of the time being requested. It is this concentration of focus on working toward measurable results that is driving our public service arena forward.

* * *

THE POWER OF DETERMINATION

Have you noticed that there is an emerging new determination to succeed among us? We are seeing it constantly exhibited at joint meetings of public service agencies. .Nowhere was it more evident than at a recent meeting of folks representing the Collaborative Regional Institute, the Regional Jobs Initiative, the Fresno Business Council and several other community-based agencies. For too long too many groups have been too content to just go through the motions when it comes to superficially trying to improve our economic, social and civic environment. There is now a commitment in the countenance of each attendee. There is an underlying seriousness of purpose that has been sorely absent among veteran "committee member" types. This region is changing. Last week's meeting saw it on display.

* * *

MAKING A DIFFERENCE

I would venture the thought that there is not a public or private entity that does not use at least part its meeting agenda to review and update its ongoing aspirations. In that vein I would like to share with you a quotation I received recently from Dr. Peter Mehas, Fresno County Superintendent of Schools. "Major achievement in any field cannot be accomplished without discipline, without pain, without self-denial. We must be willing to say no to ourselves today for the sake of a better tomorrow. We must develop our capacity to postpone present gratification for future fulfillment. We must possess the courage to make choices and abide by them. We must acknowledge our own weaknesses, anticipate them, and not allow them to reign over us."

Where are we today? Where do we want to be tomorrow? Can we do more or are we already at capacity? The need is great.

It's a tough call, isn't it?

* * *

PERSONAL INTEGRITY

Remember when we used to study antonyms? Consider these: Merit/Power; Truth/Distortion; Civility/Rancor; Respect/Abuse; Education/Ignorance; Stewardship/Selfishness.

From time to time it is proper that we re-examine our core values. Each of us has established our own personal code of conduct. The challenge becomes adhering to the standard we have set for ourselves. It is this rigid creed of internal expectations that will keep our ship steady during those times when we sail through stormy and unchartered seas.

Just for the heck of it, why not write down three synonyms for the first of each of the antonyms? I'll help with the first one. Merit =esteem=excellence=quality.

Therein rests the foundation of personal integrity.

* * *

PUBLIC AGENCY EXPECTATIONS

One of the greater challenges facing public agencies is how best to maximize available resources. They are being looked to for strong leadership in ever-expanding areas of public concern. The City of Fresno's governance structure is far improved from its status only a few short years ago. Fresno City and County competitive stresses are becoming but distant memories. Campaign promises made in March are expected to be kept in November.

As a community, our task is how best to be effective in ratcheting up our desire for a more efficient, more dynamic and truly representative system of public governance.

Is that expecting too much?

* * *

WE SHALL OVERCOME

It's been more than 40 years since Dr. Martin Luther King, Jr. made "We shall overcome" a household phrase. I believe it is in a similar context that our regional community will overcome the inhibiting obstacles of internally focused and narrowly defined pursuits.

We are beginning to realize that our economic and social successes will be measured by our voluntary collaboration with each other avidly supported by those in positions of public authority. Drawing upon the passion of Dr. King, we are laying the groundwork for a historic leap forward in the economic vitality of this Great Central Valley.

We, too, shall overcome!

* * *

DISCRETIONARY TIME

One of life's biggest challenges, it seems to me, is recognizing one's personal responsibility to participate in productive community service.

I cannot but think we should be constantly looking for ways to maximize our individual opportunities through the most effective utilization of our discretionary time. The farther we travel on our life's journey as extremely busy folks, the more it becomes critical for each of us to define and accept our role in helping our extended community attain its vision.

For each of us, it is a very discretionary decision. Have you made yours?

* * *

MEMORY FROM A BACCALAUREATE SERVICE

My wife and I went to our granddaughter's university Baccalaureate Service a week ago. Here's an excerpt from the program:

"I am only one, but I am one,
I cannot do everything, but I can do something;
and what I should do and can do, by the grace of God I will do".

One of the rewards in composing these weekly "thoughts" is to silently recognize all who have accepted the commitment inherent in the quotation. To each we all owe an immense debt of respect and gratitude. We are making progress in our journey thanks to all of those who simply and without fanfare have accepted their responsibility to "do something."

* * *

PUBLIC SAFETY

COMBATING THE GANG CULTURE

Draw an X.

Where the two lines come together is our focal point in addressing the impact of the gang culture upon us. We offer congratulations to local law enforcement agencies for the support given them by Governor Schwarzenegger in an all-out commitment to stopping gang violence. Great strides are being made in the Fresno area thanks to the leadership of Police Chief Jerry Dyer and his police officers in cooperation with Fresno County Sheriff Margaret Mimms and her deputies.

Adding community support are the programs outlined in the newly released *Human Investment Initiative*. Through this farsighted program we shall increase our concentration on creating an environment for young people which will deflect the allure of gang membership. Ultimately, it will be when we focus equally upon the causes as well as the symptoms that gang culture will be overcome.

We are approaching that intersection.

* * *

CAUSES BEFORE SYMPTOMS

If there is one fundamental truth in addressing our crime problem in the Fresno Metropolitan Area, it is that the lasting solution will not come from apprehending and imprisoning the offenders. Rather, the problem will be abated when a more concentrated effort is placed upon removing the causes that lead to the symptoms. Poverty, lack of education, dysfunctional homes, joblessness, gangs, etc., all are the breeding grounds of a criminal lifestyle. Each is an area of concern that must be specifically addressed and abated. It is to our credit that we are making strides in these areas. We are realizing that we either make an adequate investment in crime prevention or we immerse ourselves in ever expanding debt paying for larger and larger prisons.

We have made our commitment. Our challenge is to make that commitment become reality.

* * *

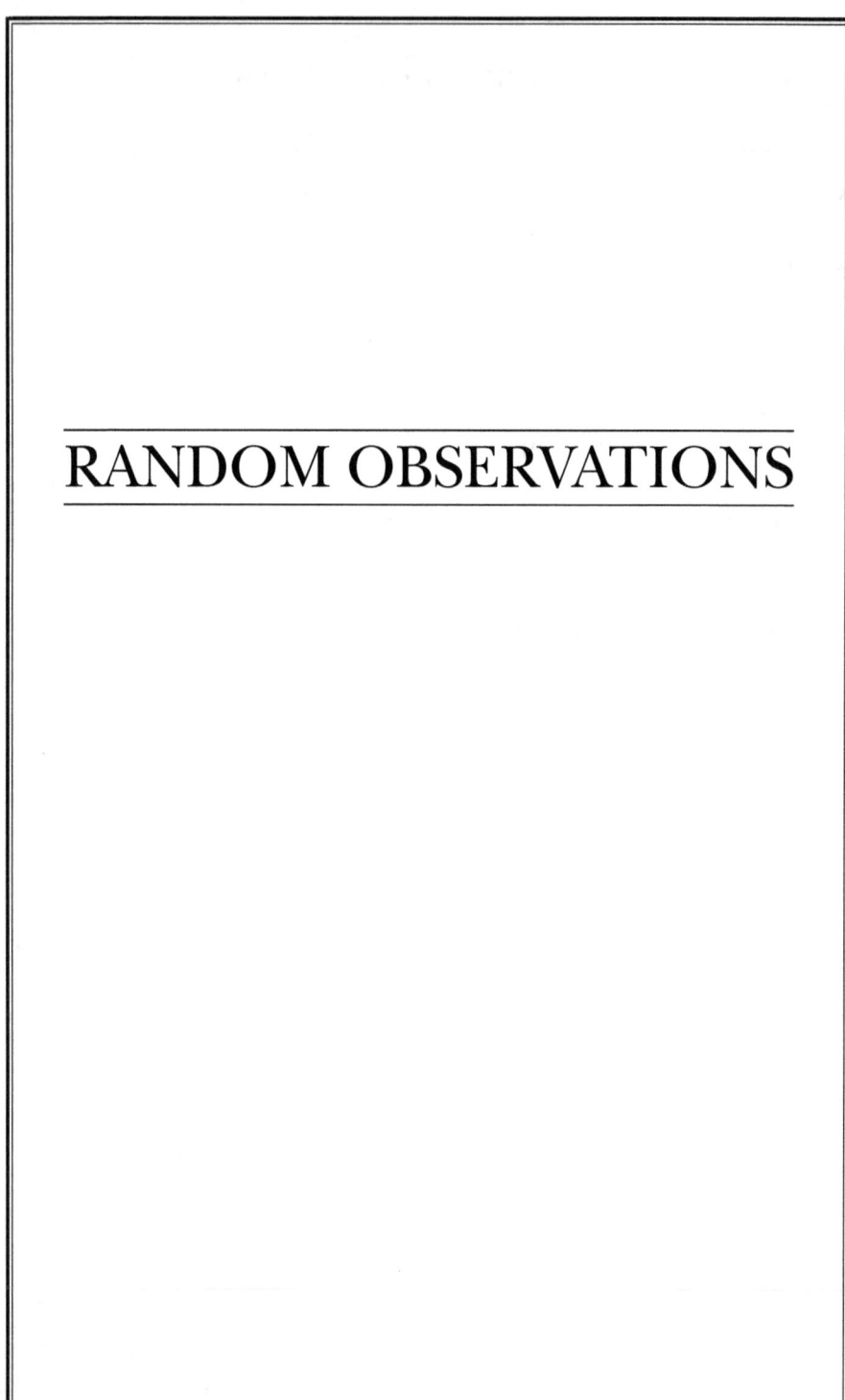

RANDOM OBSERVATIONS

A LOOK BACKWARD

Some day when a historian of our regional transformation writes our story, it is my fervent hope that the focus will be on our mission of bringing the public and private sectors into closer harmony for the betterment of all of our people. May the record describe our struggle to work toward the elimination of jurisdictional roadblocks. May we be remembered as forgoing selfishness in a search for a commonality within lofty goals coupled with a fiery zest for better ways of attaining them May history describe us as sharply focused participants devoted to a single-minded perseverance in creating growing opportunities for all regardless of social, economic or ethnic background.

Let me know how it works out.

* * *

A GOLFER'S PERSPECTIVE

Those of you who don't play golf might want to go right on by this thought!

Here is a little golfing vernacular? Does it seem to you that a lot of our trouble around here is that we have trouble sinking our putts? We seem to be pretty good at driving the ball off the tee. The fairway shots usually reflect our handicap. It's when we're on the green and it's time to sink the putt to close out the hole that we get the yips.

Does anyone have any suggestions for a solution?

* * *

THOUGHT FOR A NEW DAY

I thought you might be interested in an anonymous "Thought for a New Day" that I have had in my files for some time.

"This is the beginning of a new day. God has given me this day to use as I will. I can waste it or use it for good. What I do to-day is important, because I'm exchanging a day of my life for it. When tomorrow comes, this day will be gone forever, leaving in its place something that I have traded for it. I want it to be gain, not loss; success not failure; so that I shall not regret the price I paid for it."

Each of us needs to make an investment of ourselves this day and every day–each of us.

* * *

RELATIONSHIPS

RAISING THE LEVEL OF THE LAKE

The Fresno Business Council came into existence about six years ago based upon a fundamental premise–if we could raise the level of the water in our economic, social and cultural lake, all boats upon it would rise together. The Council's mission has been to create a spirit of collaboration, communication and dedication in such areas as job creation, education, public safety and public policy. As a result, week by week we are witnessing organizations and individuals coming forward to join with us in working for a higher and bolder broad-based standard of living for all of us. In my other life we called this "Espirit de Corps."

Our lake is rising steadily and smoothly because we are learning to sail upon it together.

* * *

AGENCY ALLIANCES

Have you sensed an increasing aura of commitment emanating from the willingness of various public and private community-based agencies to work together for the common good? New challenges by which they can maximize their impact on economic and social progress are being defined and accepted. They are enthusiastically studying this area's immediate and extended needs and jointly developing critical strategies to help meet them. Their confidence in their ability to help bring about positive change is rising. In short, they are vigorously exploring new routes to greater effectiveness.

All of this reminds me of an old adage–"Example is not the main thing in influencing others. It is the only thing."

* * *

MENTORSHIP

One of life's greatest gifts, it seems to me, is the privilege of having one or more mentors. Nowhere is mentoring a greater resource than within the realm of the activities of community-based agencies. When do we draw a line in the sand? When do we move away from our preferred position in order to bring about a consensus vital to attaining a defined goal? Difficult decisions require demanding discussions. A mentor's counseling is an invaluable asset. Fortunate indeed are those with a mentor — and all the people said "Amen"—

* * *

REGIONAL TRANSFORMATION

THE POTTER'S WHEEL

Have you ever sat at a potter's wheel pondering the formless mound of wet clay in front of you? Then the wheel begins to spin. Your hands start to mold the mud before you. What was once a blob begins to assume an identifiable shape.

Each of us has an equal opportunity to sit in the potter's chair. Together we shall mold this region's tomorrow. Regardless of our social or jurisdictional level, we live in a democracy where everyone has an opportunity to contribute to our destiny. Soft clay is malleable. As we pool our skills, so do we mold our future. Our community's potter's wheel can only produce what we create together. It is when our creation is taken from the wheel and placed in the kiln for preservation that we. ensure our destiny.

So the question then becomes whether or not each of us is taking our turn sitting at the potter's wheel.

* * *

ILLNESS TO WELLNESS

Think about this.

All of us desire to rid ourselves of our economic, educational and social Illnesses. Economic weaknesses, both in the public and private sectors, too often suffer from the afflictions of being Ill. Our educational systems have underdone a plethora of serious Illnesses and are in the process of healing. We still have a nationally recognized Illness in our social welfare system. How many of these Illnesses have remained with us because those individuals and organizations afflicted have not taken the remedial steps to become WEll? WEllness is built around the concept of looking for ways to serve the whole of which each component is an interacting and beneficial part. While some Illnesses may always be with us, the road to Wellness is at hand because those who live, work, play and pray among us are demanding an end to our historic Illness.

MAKING IT HAPPEN

We hear a lot about moving forward these days–but with a twist. No longer is creating a plan the end of an exercise. Our filing cabinets are filled to overflowing with extensively researched and dust-gathering plans of all varieties. Rather, we are now demanding that planning be coupled with providing for the initiation of those actions necessary to transform planning into reality.

It's called "Making It Happen."

* * *

BOUNDARY CROSSING

The farther we travel down the road as an extended community committed to regional transformation, the more we recognize the impact being made by our adherence to the Community Values of the Fresno Region in our decision making.

The second value is Boundary Crossing and Collaboration. *"We are willing to cross political, social, ethnic and economic boundaries and partner with others to achieve community outcomes. We will lead 'beyond the walls' to create an inclusive, cohesive community through partnership and collaboration".*

Keep this in mind the next time you hear someone pontificating that only certain components of our society are qualified to lead us!

* * *

THE TIPPING POINT

Recently many of us were privileged to hear an address recently by California State Secretary of Business, Transportation and Housing, Sunne Wright McPeak. Ms. McPeak's audience of business executives stressed that we are at a "tipping point" in creating a new era for this region after years of being short changed by our elected and bureaucratic officials in Sacramento and in Washington, D.C.

As this transformation comes about it will be because the private sector (that's us) got off of our duffs and became involved in critical decision making by our state and national office holders and are following through with action. The speaker was adamant in emphasizing that the tipping point is today. There is no substitute for business-based participation in creating effective public policy. Business leadership is fundamental to our economic and social well being. Bring on tomorrow.

* * *

TRANSFORMATION REFLECTIONS

In reflecting upon the transformational impact underway in this region over the past several years, one thing stands out. Progress occurs when folks from divergent groups and differing opinions work collaboratively in arriving at mutually beneficial decisions. We are witnessing a broad community of passionately dedicated improvement seekers serving together without demanding individual adulation. The Fresno Business Council has become the standard bearer for higher levels of organizational and individual conduct built upon its "Statement of Community Values.".

And that is worth reflecting upon.

* * *

PLANNING FOR GROWTH

One of the significant challenges of any maturing organization is to reassess constantly its most effective areas of public service.

The Fresno Business Council, for example, was created as an organization focused primarily on seeking higher economic, political and social standards for the Metropolitan Fresno area. As the years passed, it has become intimately involved in a multitude of Fresno County issues. Today, with the increasing recognition of the importance of regionalism, it is reaching a point in its life where it has broadened its scope to include an even more expanded universe. Where we were yesterday and where we are today are only reference libraries as to where we must be tomorrow.

* * *

RETURN ON INVESTMENT

In the business world we talk a lot about return on investment.

It might be well for each of us to inventory the diverse contributions being made in our ongoing regional social and economic transformation. While admittedly impossible to measure in specific dollars, the dividends from our investments are growing month by month. Why? Because of higher expectations created in an expanding enlightened collaborative environment among our dedicated private, non-profit and public sector partners. Our investment in this greater community of both our personal time and fiscal resources is there for all to see.

As for tomorrow, what's wrong with showing a profit?

* * *

REGIONALISM

THE DEFINER IS COMMITMENT

There is a new definition of determination around here. Nowhere was it more evident than at a recent meeting of a regional gathering of volunteers and staff representing a large number of community-based organizations.

For too long too many have been too content to just go through the motions when it comes to improving our economic, social and civic environment. There is now a commitment in the countenance of each attendee. There is an underlying seriousness of purpose seldom seen among veteran "committee-member" types. This region is changing because of the realization that yesterday's "cotton candy" agendas did not address tomorrow's hard copy challenges.

For those of you raised on a farm, our horse has its bit in its teeth.

* * *

TASK FORCES

One of this region's most effective contributions to community development (at least in my opinion) has been our growing ability to redefine expectations of the valuable time of our volunteer participants. We are more and more focusing on carefully created task forces designed to address specific concerns. Many members are being individually solicited because of their particular skills in strengthening the group as a whole. In addition, members from numerous other agencies are adding their expertise in helping to create solutions for chronic problems that have seemed insurmountable for far too long.

No longer are we just talking about our individual concerns. We have learned how to assemble an effective team to solve them!

Hooray for Task Forces!!

* * *

REACHING A TURNING POINT

I sense a new aura of excitement about what's going on all around us. We are witnessing a turning point in the way we are addressing our problems. Maybe not a rectangular turning point, but surely a hexagonal one! Why? Because our greater community is rapidly discovering that we can bring about a new creative atmosphere by getting ourselves personally involved.

As we go forward in this new environment, each of us in the private sector must cling to our vision of working with the public sector in a spirit of harmonious cooperation in creating more and better jobs, increased public safety and an ever stronger educational system. The opportunity is at hand, and we are grasping it.

Exciting? You betcha it is!

* * *

THE HUMAN INVESTMENT INITIATIVE

I think one of the most rewarding results of all the transformation activity that is emerging among us is the increased usage of such terms as collaboration, interaction, boundary crossing and similar expressions. Each emphasizes a fundamental pathway for effectively addressing the social and economic difficulties faced by this region.

The validity of such descriptions was dramatically confirmed at the presentation of the *Human Investment Initiative* at a well-attended recent meeting convened by the Fresno Business Council. The eclectic audience was presented with a road map out of both poverty and educational shortcomings through this "rubber on the road" approach.

The initiative is the result of months of intense effort by volunteers and staff from private, public, civic, cultural, educational and faith based organizations and agencies. Good things lie ahead because good people care enough to meet critical issues head on. The *Human Investment Initiative* will become a shining beacon in lighting our way forward.

* * *

CROSSING AN ABYSS IN A WHEELBARROW

The President of my Rotary Club recently shared a humorous little story with us that I would like to paraphrase and pass along to you in a more serious vein. It concerns the tightrope walker who pushed a wheelbarrow across Niagara Falls many times. One day he asked if anyone would like to ride along with him.

The basic news that I wish to share is that we in this region are crossing our own abyss to arrive at a better tomorrow. Even greater news is that our wheelbarrow is being pushed by scores of collaborating agencies and individuals. It is filled with exciting projects and initiatives. Education, health care, human resources, job creation, public safety, leadership training, community values—all are in the wheelbarrow. The greatest news is that there is still room behind the wheelbarrow for more pushers and within the wheelbarrow for more initiatives.

The decision for each of us is to ensure that we are either behind or in the wheelbarrow so that we aren't left behind.

* * *

BUILDING AN ARK

As we continue our journey to regional transformation, I think we need to empathize with Noah.

We have been building an ark. We are now ready to cast off the anchor that holds us to our present mooring. We are ready to sail for a new horizon, a new sense of expectation, and a new standard in public/private collaboration.

Now we are faced with the real challenge. Do we have everyone on board? From the elephants to the ants and all in between, it is imperative that no one is left behind. Together with all of our ship-builders and crew, we must ensure the success of our endeavor by making certain that our passenger list is comprised of visionaries of an inclusive community.

All ashore that wish to go ashore! Raise the gangway, shipmates. It's time to embark upon an exciting voyage together.

* * *

SEASONS OF THE YEAR

WELCOME TO SPRINGTIME

Do you like allegories? Every winter the long awaited rainfall this area receives supplies much of the critical underground moisture needed to sustain our dormant plants, bushes and trees. In the months that follow, this below-the-surface energy bursts forth into lush fields of green grasses, vivid swatches of spectacular wildflowers and a stunning array of fragrant and colorful tree blossoms on our mountainsides and in our valleys.

An allegory tells us that, as an extended community, we are carefully nourishing the below-the-surface energy of this region's cultural and economic soil. We have added nutrients by strengthening alliances and formulating effective policies and programs designed to ensure a better tomorrow for all among us. This region's vision is to realize our potential for greatness in this fertile valley by effectively converting the quietly accumulated energy of wintertime into the productiveness of an invigorated dynamic springtime.

Exciting days are ahead of us.

* * *

HELLO SUNSHINE – GOODBYE FOG

During the late springtime of the year when the sun shines warmly is a strange time to be thinking of winter's fog. But the thought came to me that this community is beginning to grasp the realism that if we are ever to come together, we must do so in the bright sunshine of collaboration and not in the shadowy gloominess of self-centeredness. Daily we hear of new and exciting examples of individuals and groups reaching out to each other and vowing that by working cooperatively things can be different.

We welcome all that are joining with us in saying hello to the springtime sunshine and goodbye to the wintertime fog.

SPRINGTIME BEAUTY

Do you want to give yourself a real treat? Take a ride with family or friends up into our Sierra foothills this very day if possible. Never have the hills been so covered with flowers—whites, oranges, purples, blues, yellows—all resting upon a blanket of vivid green grasses and looked down upon by mountain tops capped with gleaming white snow.

To me it is an inspiring reminder that even though the majestic oaks may still be slumbering in their wintertime dormancy, there is bursting forth the eternal promise of springtime. If we shall only take the time to recognize the contribution made by the little flowers standing together in their beds of beauty, we shall not be overawed when the giant trees awake from their winter nap.

I think there is a parable in this thought someplace. I hope you agree.

* * *

SUMMERTIME'S IMPETUS

Here's something to keep your eye on. Every year about this time we drive two stakes in the ground entitled "the start of summer" and "the end of summer."

For too many years, most of us have had a tendency to excuse ourselves from significant volunteer public effort during the hot summer months. Lately, however, we have been witnessing an ever increasing year around private sector commitment to community involvement. At the same time, through the ballot box, we are demanding higher year around performance standards from our public officials. The culmination of the combination is creating accelerated expectations of a significantly stronger regional economy. Such activity allows no time for a summer hiatus.

Keep your eye on the activity between the stakes this year.

* * *

GOODBYE TO SUMMER

We're once again wrapping up the "good old summertime." It's time to welcome September and the optimism of fall's harvest of activities. It's that period of the year when we need to take time to reassess our values and establish, reestablish, or refine our goals for the upcoming months. With so many challenges (and challenges are opportunities) before us, each of us can reexamine our contribution to our extended community's agenda. Ultimately, it is up to each of us individually to decide what our contribution will be to our upcoming harvest.

Have you decided?

* * *

FALL'S FULLFILLMENT

It seems only yesterday that we were welcoming the multi-colored springtime blossoms adorning this valley's spectacular display of fruit orchards. All too soon we are equally enthralled by the vivid yellows, oranges and reds of their falling leaves as autumn arrives.

The true beauty of our landscape lies not in these vivid outer displays of elegance but inside the trees themselves. When a seedling is planted, great care is given to the fertility of the soil to sustain its life and proper nutrients to promote its growth. It is this inner source of energy that is the critical requirement for its later ability to bear marketable fruit. Our core values, our respect for our contemporaries, and our willingness to work with all who are like-minded comprise the soil from which we have sprung. Regardless of outward dissimilarities, it is our collective inner vitality that is producing a bountiful harvest. That process has no season.

* * *

AUTUMN'S INVIGORATION

It's probably non supportable, but it seems to me that with the invigorating change in the weather as fall approaches, there also occurs an invigorating change in our determination to bring about a regional transformation in this valley. Is there a correlation between cooling temperatures and warming enthusiasm for participation in creating a better tomorrow? What's the connection between falling leaves and a rising commitment to community concerns? How do you connect bundling up for frosty mornings and stripping down for heated involvement?

Just thought I'd ask.

* * *

FALL HARVEST

With the fall agricultural harvest in full swing, I cannot but dwell upon the ongoing and potential harvest of community improvement because of the dedicated efforts of so many individuals and organizations.

Think about this for a minute. A business incubator; an educational system study commission; a juvenile justice system/private sector alliance, downtown revitalization, a community needs survey, a public office candidate forum—just to name a few—are all on our plate. Despite all of these concerns, it seems to me that we still have the capacity to plant and harvest additional crops. Our challenge is to utilize effectively the talents available to us.

* * *

SAVORING A NEW CULTURE

CREATING A MURAL

Stand aside Taos. There's a new kind of "colony" on our block. Rather than an "art colony," I would submit that we are creating a "regional enhancement" colony around here.

Our soil is nurturing newly sprouted, as well as stately mature, associations of varied descriptions dedicated to improving specific areas of societal concerns. Further, we have "one-upped" our New Mexico friends. Rather than maintaining the home town individuality of our efforts as they do, we are leveraging our talents in creating an inspiring regional mosaic in which everyone is in the same picture.

Is this artistically and culturally chic or what?

* * *

ADAPTING TO CHANGE

You know what I think is the hardest barrier to break down as we witness all of the progress going on all around us? It's being willing to adapt to change. It's moving out of our individual comfort zones into new ways of doing things. It's having the courage to venture with others into uncharted waters. It's having the fortitude to accept creativity as a value added asset to progress.

We are witnessing the dawn of significant change in the way we address and solve problems. One day we shall look back and take pride in what is transpiring about us. One day we shall say "I remember when" and be thankful that we placed tomorrow ahead of yesterday.

* * *

LISTENING

I would like to share an observation with you.

Last week I had the privilege of attending three meetings comprised of leaders from throughout our greater community all concerned with development—economic, social and spiritual. For quite awhile now we have been talking to each other about collaboration.

So what's difference? I think we're beginning to listen to each other.

* * *

TO MY STERLING SILVER FRIENDS

While attending a conference recently I came across something that I would like to share with you:

"To My Sterling Silver Friends—
There is a big difference between a sterling silver plate
and a silver-plated one.
One is silver all the way through and is expensive.
The other is silver on the outside only and costs less.
The silver on the plated plate can wear off fast.
The copper or metal underneath soon shows through."

It may take more time to recognize the sterling person than the silver-plated one. You have to see this person in successes, failures, hopes and dreams, disappointments and joys. Yes, like silver, it costs more to be a sterling person. It demands much more in terms of integrity, honesty, unselfishness and patience.

It also defines the meaning of an abiding friendship among friends composed of sterling silver.

* * *

SWEDISH HARMONY

I was reminded the other day of an old Swedish proverb that says "You can't have harmony if everyone plays the same note."

As each of us discovers our place as a member of a harmonious coalition of entities working toward the betterment of our community, it is important that we recognize the differences between disagreement and discord, between mutual respect for differing opinions and disrespect for alternative presentations, between dignity and coarseness.

As we develop and present our considered solutions toward the resolution of some of our economical and societal problems, let us hope that they will be accepted in the spirit of Swedish harmony.

* * *

SEARCHING FOR SOLUTIONS

TOMORROW'S THINKERS

If there is one basic criterion for success in today's business world, it is that tomorrow's requirements will not be met with yesterday's thinking. One of my great satisfactions has been witnessing the recognition and admiration of tomorrow's progressive thinkers among us who serve either in career or elected public positions. These farsighted individuals work within an environment too easily polluted by those entrenched in archaism.

To the men and women in positions of public service who have the vision and the skills fundamental to meeting tomorrow's challenges despite these difficulties, this little thought is dedicated.

* * *

BECOMING EFFECTIVE

Here's an intriguing thought. President James Madison (1751-1836) said: "The great definer is not what we have learned but what we have become". It has taken us a while, but we're getting there.

More and more we are viewing studies, surveys, plans, and similar efforts not to be worthy of the energy expended in creating them unless the information gathered can be seamlessly segued into a real world solution to the subject matter addressed. "Learning" creates value only when it can be translated into "Becoming."

We are "Becoming."

* * *

THE NEW MILLENIUM

GRATITUDE AT A CENTURY'S END

It's finally upon us—the end of a century. What is an appropriate expression at a time like this? One of my biggest weekly challenges in expressing a thought to those who receive the Fresno Business Council's Weekly Bulletin has been to make an observation or two worthy of the reader's attention. Truthfully, I have been approaching this week with apprehension—my last shared thought of this century. We shall enter the new millennium with redefined goals and a new energy to accomplish them. There will be plenty of time to comment upon them in the upcoming weeks and months. So, let me conclude this century in an attitude of gratitude.

Thanks for granting me the privilege of being a member of an organization dedicated to placing the betterment of the whole ahead of individual recognition.

Thanks to all of our members who have given so generously of their time and talent so vital to the success of our quest.

Thanks to all of those who have joined with the Fresno Business Council in a collaborative effort enforced by the realization that together we can accomplish what none of us could do alone.

Thanks to those public officials who have placed civic improvement at the top of their priority list and welcomed the efforts of this Council and others to join with them in the pursuit of a better life for all among us.

Thanks to all of our educators who have accepted our constructive concerns about their enormous responsibilities.

Thanks to those dedicated nonprofit and public service staff members along with all of those community-minded volunteers without whom we could not have accomplished what we have and with whom we eagerly accept the challenges of tomorrow.

Finally, thanks to our Deity, however perceived, under whose ultimate supreme governance we toil.

* * *

THE ROAD TO SUCCESS

CATCH THE SPIRIT

The spirit of change is surrounding us with justified excitement. Check out construction of the city of Fresno's new downtown stadium.

By next spring, we shall witness the addition of the finishing touches on a baseball/soccer/concert complex that will complete the transformation of a barren field into a regional edifice in which we may all take pride.

In a related sense, we are well into the process of creating a new "here" all about us. We have drafted a collaborative regional blueprint. We have identified and installed public/private relationships to build upon. We're now well into erecting the framework upon which tomorrow's economic and social finishing touches will be affixed.

There's a new "can do" spirit in the air and we're right in the middle of it.

* * *

YES WE CAN

One of the great assets of those dedicated to measurable change is their commitment to a positive approach. A prime example is the leadership of the Fresno Business Council. The Council came into existence based upon a belief that a relatively small group of dedicated business men and women could, in collaboration with others of like commitment both in and out of governmental affairs, create a better quality of life for the entire region. Part of the quest is learning how to traverse emotional highs and lows whether individually or organizationally. It is imperative that we don't let periodic injections of negativity deter us from our vision.

This great Central Valley shall one day become a crown jewel in this nation's tiara. It will happen because a concerned group of folks focused on "yes, we can" rather than "no, we can't."

123

POURING THE CONCRETE

A dear friend of mine once counseled *"Don't pour the concrete until you see where the people are walking."*

This place is deeply involved in the concrete-pouring business. As we have developed our goals and the strategies for attaining them, we have discovered where new paths must be created and are developing roadbeds for them. Agencies, both public and private, committees, task forces, and individual alliances are all a vital part of this exciting undertaking. Because of this singleness of purpose, this region is helping to create new highways on the economic road map of this area.

One thing we are learning is this: *"Go the extra mile. There are no traffic jams."*

* * *

TRACTION IS THE ANSWER

I've been rethinking the numerous activities of the Fresno Business Council since its inception in 1993. Apart from the specific programs themselves, I think the Council owes its effectiveness to one basic lesson learned in any high school physics class.

Regardless of how you load any vehicle, it won't move unless the tires "grip the road." In promoting innovative projects, public-private partnerships, non-profit networking, and high ethical conduct, its goal has always been to eliminate "slippage" (aka wasted time and energy). Its dues paying members are all paying passengers aboard a conveyance that will transport us all into the future with confidence and excitement.

Most important of all, its programs have traction. Somebody once said: *"Who cares if we care? Everybody cares. Caring without action is nothing. Caring with action is everything."*

Caring with traction is contagious, isn't it?

* * *

OUR GLASS: HALF FULL OR HALF EMPTY?

Has it occurred to you that many of our current problems as we near the end of 1994 have arisen from a mind set that looks at every glass as being half empty?

Why do we as a community too often view everything negatively? When are we going to establish attainable goals and create the will to achieve them? When are we going to realize that our glass is half full? We can have a revitalized downtown Fresno with all of its positive spin-offs. We can have a business incubator for aspiring entrepreneurs. We can have safer neighborhoods. We can have more jobs for our residents. We can have better education for our children.

Isn't it time to quit this business of nay saying and state simply "We can do it so let's get after it"?

* * *

BE ALL THAT YOU CAN BE

Hold up your hand if you have heard the Army's catchy recruitment ditty, "Be All That You Can Be."

What if that became the slogan of this area? How would that affect all of the stuff going on about creating a downtown center for all kinds of activities including professional baseball, concerts, soccer, high school sporting events, etc? How would that affect land use development such as proposed by the Growth Alternatives Alliance? How would that affect the way education is delivered? It seems to me that we are still seeking the commitment for our future proposed by the Army recruitment jingle.

Why can't we be "All That We Can Be"? What stands in our way? Let's sign up!

* * *

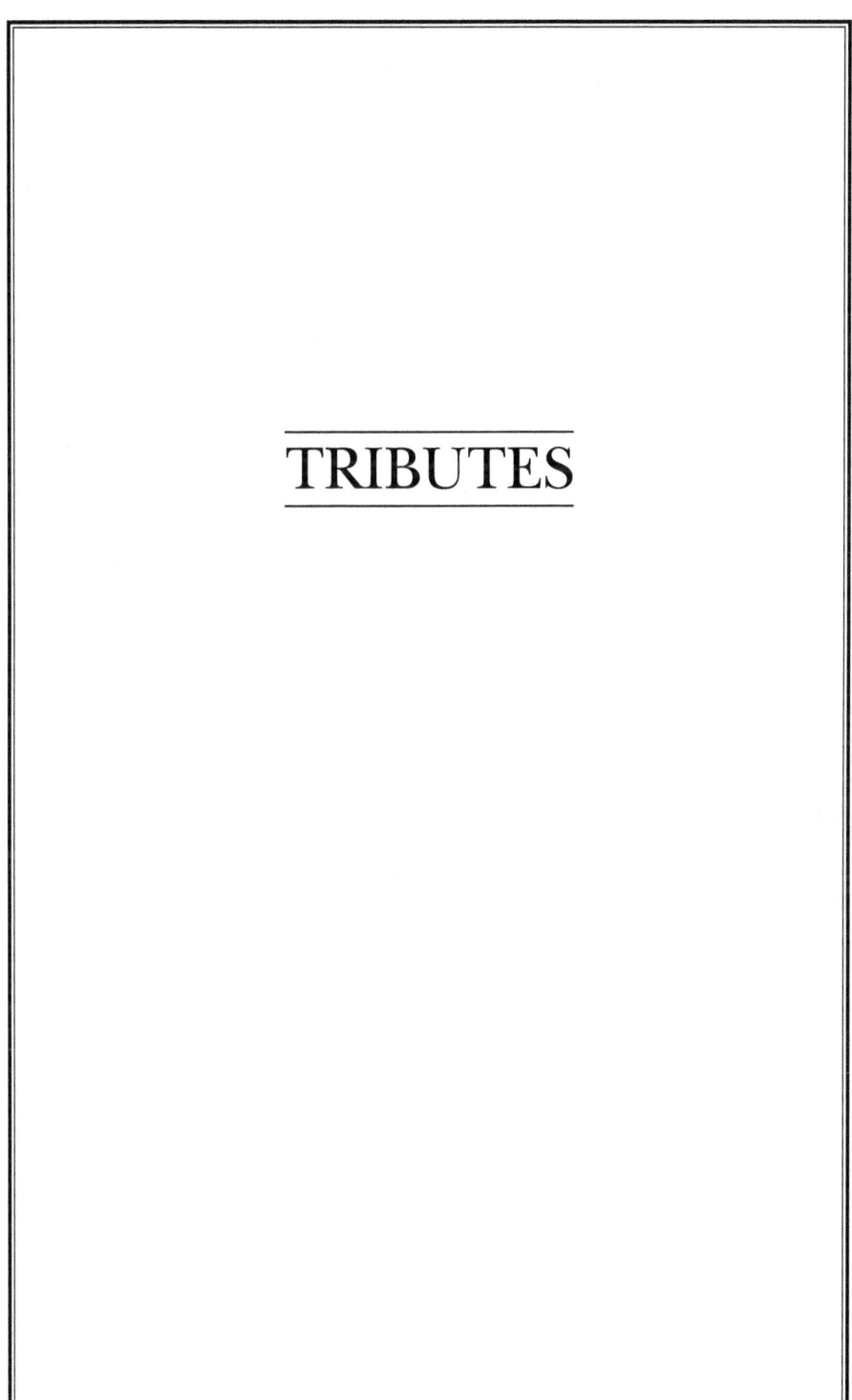

TRIBUTES

A TRIBUTE TO CHARACTER

Thirteen years ago the Fresno Business Council was established. The congealer that brought the founders together was strengthening the stewardship connection between those with public authority and the community at large. Public officials were all too often lackeys whose primary function was self promotion and obeying the wishes of the power brokers supporting them. Personal integrity had become secondary to seeking and retaining positional perks.

We were recently given another example of the insidiousness of such a system. Rather than giving in to political pressure to vote against his conscience, our State Assemblyman, Juan Arambula, voted in a manner in keeping with his academic, political and moral standards. For that he was vilified by the Assembly leadership. For shame! It reminds me of a quotation from Mahatma Gandhi – "Be the change you want to see in the world" This is the same change envisioned by the Fresno Business Council thirteen years ago.

Thank you, Juan, for supporting our mission through your action.

E-MAIL APPRECIATION

What if we made this "E-Mail Appreciation Week" to say thanks to those among us who work so diligently to make things better around here?

All about us are dedicated givers of their time and substance by participating on Boards of Directors, task forces and committees of organizations whose primary reason for existence is to be a part of creating a better community. Most of these efforts are performed quietly without a thirst for individual recognition.

Why not take a few minutes to e-mail someone and tell him or her how much you appreciate their efforts on behalf of all of the rest of us? Just hit the "send" key.

A SALUTE TO EDUCATORS

Will all of our educators stand up please!

Whether it's called graduation, matriculation, commencement or certification, diploma time is the time of the year when many of today's students find themselves one step closer to becoming tomorrow's job holders. Their success in life will be determined to a great extent by the quality of their formal education. Ultimately, without the input of the professional skills of our school administrators, professors and teachers, our regional and national economy is vulnerable.

So, in our continuing search for those with the abilities to lead us to a brighter future, let's pause for a moment to salute those educators among us whose careers are dedicated to assuring us of the academic qualifications of those students they are passing on to us.

They may all sit down now.

* * *

DEATH OF POPE JOHN PAUL II

Last week the world came together, if only for a brief time. Political issues and personal agendas were temporarily set aside to honor the memory of Pope John Paul II. From the most noted to the most humble, individuals from all walks of life paused and commemorated the life of this complex, yet simple, man.

It is appropriate that our thoughts reflect upon his passing also. In a world filled with divisiveness on so many seemingly complex earthly and spiritual issues, last week's unity of tribute to a departed denominational patriarch underscores an old adage. *"The Greatness of Anyone Can Nearly Always Be Measured By Their Willingness to Be Kind"*.

* * *

INSPIRATION BY EXAMPLE

Last week this region caught a vision of the challenges and rewards of servant leadership and recognized the services of those imbued with rock-solid ethics and outstanding achievement in public life. Congratulations to Fresno Pacific University for convening their annual Business Forum breakfast featuring the esteemed author and lecturer Mr. Ken Blanchard. His enthusiastic remarks to a capacity audience called us all to a higher standard in leading our community's economic and social development.

Likewise, The Fresno Bee, the Maddy Institute and the Fresno Business Council once again shined a spotlight on those in elected positions who emulate the character of the late Senator Rose Ann Vuich. Also honored were those in professional public service careers whose performances set the bar by which others are measured. Congressman Cal Dooley and Great Valley Center President Carol Whiteside were most deserving award winners at the presentation luncheon.

One of life's greatest gifts, in my opinion, is the gift of being inspired by others. Last week hundreds of us we were once again inspired to seek new levels in the conduct of our own lives through the examples placed before us by our public heroes.

* * *

DO THE MATH

Try this bit of mental exercise. Make a wild guess at the number of volunteer hours being donated to community based programs every month around here. How much time is donated to researching and preparing those valuable documents dedicated to showing us ways to better ourselves? How much time is donated to a multitude of nonprofit Boards and Advisory Groups? Whether it is individually or as part of an organized agency, we need to give recognition to the dedicated men and women who form the backbone of the transformation going on around us.

What is this worth? As I see it, the value is priceless, simply because it is a gift.

* * *

TENDING THE GARDEN

As our gardens, hills and fields begin to brighten our landscape with the flowers of springtime, I am reminded once again of a little plaque located on the grounds of my mother and father's final earthly residence. "Everyone loves a garden, but few will step off its paths to cultivate it."

I think we need to take some time to extend our thanks to those gardeners who are carefully nurturing our common soil. Their efforts to seek new ways to sow the seeds, raise the plants and gather in striking bouquets of measurable community progress for all of us are deserving of our highest praise. We all know who they are, from the most visible to those who prefer to work quietly in the shadow of others. Each has stepped off the pathway into the flower bed to till the soil in order to bring this beautiful emerging landscape to us. May we never forget to express our gratitude to them.

* * *

A CHRISTmas HOLIday TRIBUTE, 2005

Whether we call it CHRISTmas day or a HOLIday, this is the time of year we come together to rededicate ourselves to our mission. It is fitting that we take time to meditate about all of those who are giving so much in our noble climb up our community's mountain of transformation. I applaud all of those who have accepted the challenge of scaling the lofty peaks of collaboration, understanding and commitment. These outstanding leaders are our "sherpas" guiding us upward to a better tomorrow.

In the spirit of this Holy Season, I leave you with the moving words etched in granite on President Ronald Reagan's memorial: *"I Know In My Heart That Man Is Good, That What Is Right Will Always Eventually Triumph, And There Is Purpose And Worth To Each And Every Life."*

* * *

AN EARNED TRIBUTE, 1996

As we enter the last weeks of this year I think it is permissible if we let our emotions show a bit. Oftentimes it is considered unseemly to be overly effusive (or for that matter, overly unresponsive) about matters of close concern to us.

The Fresno Business Council has been deeply involved in many issues since its formation only three years ago. It has participated in a number of successes including being an integral part of a changing political environment around here. It is the lead dog in the formation of the soon to be established business incubator. It is the co-sponsor of an intensive investigation into the way education is delivered in this county. It is developing a new approach to matters of juvenile justice that will be finalized in the coming months. There are others.

My point is this. Let's use the next few weeks to let our emotions of gratitude shine brightly on all who have worked so diligently to bring us to this meaningful time of the year on such a high plane. High on this list are those associated with the Fresno Business Council.

* * *

TRUST

THE CANARY ON MY SHOULDER

The little yellow bird that sits on my shoulder whispered to me the other day and asked: "what's the most important word in anyone's language?" After a lot of thought I think I have the answer.

It is TRUST. Whether it is faith, family, friends, or our "work-a-day world" relationships, everything eventually succeeds or fails based upon trust or lack thereof. Each of our lives through its many spin offs and alliances confirms this. Our ability to discuss personal matters with our confidants confirms this. Our loving relationship with our spouses, our children and grandchildren confirms this. Our anticipation of spending happy hours with friends confirms this.

I can hardly wait to hear what my little canary has to say next. I'll let you know. Trust me!

* * *

TRUST IS THE KEY

The more one searches for the driving force behind all of the positives surrounding the superlative community contributions of so many around here, the more one concludes that it is all based upon a single word. Trust is the key.

We are learning to trust one another's principles as the bedrock of one another's actions. We are recognizing that without mutual trust lasting progress is but an illusive dream. Where this relationship does not exist lies discord. No agreement can be as fragile as one lacking mutual trust by the parties. Nothing can be as enduring as one based upon simple trust.

* * *

TRUST – OR THE LACK OF IT

Among organizations dedicated to working together to enhance their effectiveness, one of the frustrations remains the occasional groups and individuals who feel threatened by trusting one another. Rather than lowering their castle's drawbridges and draining their moats, there still remain those who would close the gates and add more and larger alligators. It is to our greater community's credit that such instances are becoming increasingly rare. Trust and credibility are the foundation blocks upon which we are building our tomorrows—and that's as it should be!

* * *

VACATION MUSINGS

TRAVEL AS A REALITY CHECK

Have you ever equated foreign travel to an introspective reality check?

One of the greatest risks in being so focused upon improving our regional quality of life here at home is forgetting how fortunate we are today in comparison with so many others elsewhere. It is only necessary to journey out of our bountiful nation to fully appreciate our present economic, educational and cultural gifts and the opportunities we have as free men and women to improve them.

One doesn't have to travel far to make appreciating the United States of America a very real heart-awakening experience.

* * *

RIVER RAFTING

Recently my brothers and I shared an eleven-day river rafting experience in northern Canada. Drifting along is easy when the river is wide and the water is calm. But when the channel narrows, and the swiftness of the rapids increase, it becomes increasingly important that all of those aboard synchronize their paddling to avoid smashing into the rocks.

It seems to me that we are now in the middle of our own rapids here at home in faster and faster waters. How we coordinate our efforts will determine the condition of our raft and ourselves when we reach the smoother waters that await us down river.

It's important that we paddle together. Don't fall overboard.

* * *

CULTURAL CONTEMPLATION

As you read this, I shall be somewhere between Korea and Japan with one of my brothers as the only two passengers on a mega container ship bound from Hong Kong to Long Beach.

There is nothing that makes one more aware of what we have at home than comparing our country's multicultural immigrant-based population with those primarily one nationality countries elsewhere. It is this dramatic and forceful awareness of our free and diverse democratic society, albeit far from perfect, that is in striking contrast to the single cultural environment so prevalent abroad. As we sail from Asia bound for California, you may be sure that once again I am giving thanks for the opportunity to live in our great nation.

* * *

HOME IS A GEMSTONE

One of the great things about international travel is developing a greater appreciation of home.

As my brothers and I conclude our annual sea voyage together as the only passengers on a containership that called at seven ports in four South American countries, Fresno, California, becomes a gemstone. Our system of government, imperfect as it sometimes seems, is a gemstone. Our ability to recognize cultural and economic differences and work together to alleviate them is a gemstone. Our compassion and our compulsion to help those in need throughout the world is a gemstone. Our faith in God is a gemstone.

Our individual challenge is to join with those about us in protecting these precious assets as we collaboratively strive to enhance their home grown value.

* * *

TRAVEL AS AN EDUCATOR

I am composing this as my two brothers and I are enroute from Charleston, S.C. to Chile as the only passengers aboard a 634' containership. While transiting the Panama Canal, an image occurred to me that I would like to share with you.

The greater Fresno region is becoming nationally recognized as a canal builder. We have been instrumental in constructing a Communication Canal between the Public Sector on one side and the Private Sector on the other. No longer do voyagers on either side meet only in the stormy waters below "Cape Forlorn." Today both sides comfortably cross the narrow isthmus between them to exchange information and offer each other assistance beneficial to both.

Is that "strait" talk or what?

* * *

POST-TRAVEL REFLECTIONS

Sometimes one needs to get away from the trees to appreciate the beauty of the forest.

After three weeks of travel in several foreign countries among diverse peoples, I return with a deeper understanding of what makes this Central Valley such a special place in the world. To contrast the apparently insurmountable problems facing so many peoples in other lands with the surmountable obstacles we are determined to overcome in our part of the world is of itself inspiring. To have the privilege to know and work with so many talented unselfish individuals determined to make our collaborative transformation successful is to grasp the deeper meaning of "home."

It's good to be back among our own trees.

* * *

A VIEW FROM GREECE

My wife and I recently returned home from a "continuing education" sojourn to Greece. We were scheduled to attend a lecture on social and economic development by a fellow named Socrates, but when we arrived we learned that he has passed away.

It doesn't take much more than staring at the ruins of what at one time was a flourishing society to gain a deeper appreciation of the importance of protecting and improving our own system of government. Without being overly dramatic, our alternative is realizing that someday people will travel far distances to view our ruins. Nothing is more critical to creating a better tomorrow than determining the qualifications and dedication of those selected to lead us today.

I am sure that's what Socrates would have told us. What's your thought?

* * *

TRAVEL MEDITATIONS

Does "absence makes the heart grow fonder"? You bet it does.

Sailing leisurely across the Pacific Ocean on a Container Ship for seventeen days is an ideal setting in which to refocus one's objectives. To fully understand what we have, and to fully grasp what we can have, one needs only time for quiet reflection. There is no better meditation platform than the stern of an ocean freighter in the middle of a vast sea.

Absence does make our senses more acute. One has time to inhale the invigorating aroma of our common commitment to bringing about an improved regional economic environment. You can almost touch and taste the excitement and determination among those who will lead in keeping our region's ship on course. Positive change is upon us. It's a great time to be a traveler.

* * *

THE REWARDS OF TRAVEL

Not long ago my wife and I left for a wonderful trip visiting Berlin, Prague, Vienna and Budapest with a few stops in between. It was inspiring to see what these people have done to reconstruct their cities from near total demolition incurred in WW11. To see buildings restored to their original historical facades, to stroll down busy malls, to enjoy lunch in charming downtown sidewalk cafes, is to realize the importance of everyone's "place." To grasp the devotion with which these people restored their hopes for their future contributes to a profound desire to experience these exciting attributes here at home.

While there is no "one size fits all" formula for civic transformation, there does exist among many of us the will and the wisdom to create a new tomorrow for ourselves and those who will follow us..

Will our efforts be successful? Stay tuned.

* * *

EPILOGUE

And so we come to the end of an extended series of "Thoughts" assembled over a long number of years. It is my wish that these expressions of concern, praise, tribute, hope and prayer may inspire those who read them to create an epistle of their own to share with others.

Finally, I would like to leave you with a poem that has become my mantra as I have been privileged to be a small part of our region's efforts to create a better life for all who reside among us. I ask that the reader excuse the male gender and look instead into the heart of the feminine writer. Herein you will find what I believe to be the motivation driving all those who are working so diligently today on behalf of those who will follow them tomorrow.

* * *

THE BRIDGE BUILDER
by Will Allen Dromgoole – 1860-1934

An old man walking on life's highway
Came at evening cold and grey
To a chasm vast and deep and wide;
The old man crossed in the twilight dim
The sullen stream had no fear for him;
He turned when safe on the other side
And built a bridge to span the tide.

"Old man", said a fellow pilgrim near,
"You're wasting your strength with building here.
Your journey will end with the ending day
You never again will pass this way,
You've crossed this chasm vast and wide
Why build this bridge at eventide?"

The builder lifted his old grey head.
"Good friend, in the path I have come", he said,
"There followed after me today
A youth whose feet must pass this way.
This chasm which was naught to me
To this fair-haired youth may a pitfall be.

He, too, must cross in the twilight dim.
Good friend, I am building this bridge for him."

* * *

Community Values of the Fresno Region

Stewardship – We will lead and follow as stewards of our region, caring responsibly for our community assets. We will work together to achieve the greatest, long-term benefit for the community as a whole.

Boundary Crossing and Collaboration –We are willing to cross political, social ethnic and economic boundaries and partner with others to achieve community outcomes. We will lead "beyond the walls" to create an inclusive, cohesive community through partnership and collaboration.

Commitment to Outcomes – We are willing to take responsibility for tasks and achieving specified outcomes. We are committed to staying involved until the tasks are completed.

"Art of the Possible" Thinking – We believe that anything is possible in the Fresno Region. We will envision "success without limitations" and then backward map a specific, attainable strategy for achieving that vision.

Fact-Based Decision Making – To the greatest extent possible, we will base decisions and action plans on objective data, thereby avoiding distortion of issues by personal feelings or agendas.

Truth Telling – We value the empowerment of everyone involved, along with all community stakeholders, to honestly and forthrightly share all knowledge, experiences and insights relative to the work at hand. We take responsibility for ensuring our "truth" is current, not historical. We all share the responsibility for maintaining the truth telling standard.

Power Parity – We respect all persons and recognize that there are diverse viewpoints. Positional power will not determine a strategy or preferred outcome, merit will. Viewpoints from diverse con-stituencies will be proactively sought to ensure the best possible outcomes for the community.

Commitment to Resolving Conflict – Conflict is inevitable and is some-times required in order to achieve the best outcomes possible. Healthy conflict involves valuing every individual regardless of his or her stance on a specific issue and an unwavering commitment to working through the conflict in a positive manner despite its severity.

Asset-Based Approach – We are focused on using a strengths-based, asset-oriented approach to people and issues. We believe that posi-tive change occurs when we appreciate, value and invest in what is best in our people and community.

Conflict of Interest - We agree to disclose any personal or professional conflict of interest that may affect our objectivity before engaging in work that will impact the community. We seek to avoid even the appearance of impropriety.

ABOUT THE AUTHOR

Richard A. "Dick" Johanson was born in Fresno, California, and has been a lifelong resident of Fresno County except for his tour of duty with the United States Marine Corps in World War II where he served at Pearl Harbor, Guam and China.

He holds an Associate in Arts degree from Reedley College (Distinguished Alumnus), a Bachelor of Business Administration Degree from Armstrong University (Distinguished Alumnus of the Decade, 1940-1950) and an Honorary Doctor of Humane Letters Degree from California State University, Fresno.

He is the founder and current board chairman of Johanson Transportation Service, a nationwide major freight brokerage firm with regional offices throughout the United States. The company is currently expanding its operations internationally under the leadership of his son, Larry Johanson.

In addition to his professional career, the author has devoted much of his life to community activities. He is past chair of the Greater Fresno Chamber of Commerce; a past chair of the Fresno Metropolitan Museum (Emeritus Member); a founder, past president and past chair of the Fresno Business Council (Chair Emeritus); past chair of the Business Advisory Council, CSUF Craig School of Business (Emeritus Member). He has served on numerous other community-based boards including Fresno Pacific University Board of Trustees, CSUF Foundation Board of Governors (Emeritus Member), Marjorie Mason Center Board of Governors, Community Hospitals of Central California Foundation and Corporate Affairs boards, Fresno Philharmonic Board of Governors, Community Colleges of Central California Foundation Board of Governors, United Way Board of Governors, the Fresno Unified School District Board of Trustees (past chair), Rotary Club of Fresno (past club president and past district governor).

He has been married to his wife, Althea, for 59 years and currently resides in Clovis, California. He and Althea have two children, Larry (wife Patti) and Gale (husband Jason), and three granddaughters, Amanda, Yvonne (husband James) and Jody.

Dick is the author of "A Passion for Stewardship"-the story of his life as a member of the "Greatest Generation."

rajoho@comcast.net